CW00503442

A Voyage Round My Life

A Voyage Round My Life

Henry Boylan

Henry Boylan

To Jenny.

A. & A. Farmar

British Library cataloguing in Publication Data
A CIP catalogue record for this book is available from the
British Library.

Cover design by Alice Campbell
Text edited, designed and set by A. & A. Farmar
Printed and bound by GraphyCems

The publishers and author would like to thank Séamus Heaney and Faber &
Faber for kind permission to reproduce 'Wolfe Tone' from *The Haw Lantern*
(London 1987).

ISBN 1-899047-78-6

First published in 2002
by
A. & A. Farmar
Beech House
78 Ranelagh Village
Dublin 6
Ireland
Tel: + 353 1 496 3625
Fax: + 353 1 497 0107
Email: afarmar@iol.ie
Web: farmarbooks.com

By the same author

A Dictionary of Irish Biography (1978,
1988, 1998)

Wolfe Tone (1981)

This Arrogant City (1984)

A Valley of Kings, The Boyne (1988)

White Sails Crowding (1994)

Contents

1 The Old Man

I was born in Drogheda in December 1911, and lived there until I was nineteen, when I went to work in Dublin. There were nine of us children. I was the fourth boy, and third youngest in the family.

We lived in Riverside, a detached, three-bedroom, Georgian house on the North Strand, not far from the Boyne Viaduct. The front wall was nearly two feet thick and a stout beam was housed in it on one side of the front door. This beam was drawn out at night and slotted in a receiving aperture on the opposite side. It would have taken a battering ram to force an entry. Across the road in front of the house an open grass-covered park of about three or four acres stretched from the Viaduct to a high wall behind which were coal yards. A narrow road leading under the Viaduct into Donors Green separated this grassy space from the Ballast Quay and the river. We played cricket on it on summer days.

There was much activity on the river, and with long, deserted beaches within easy reach, every day was busy with pleasure and excitement. The woods and hedges along the banks of the river teemed with bird-life and we spent long spring afternoons bird's-nesting.

My father's family, the Boylans, were seafarers, Master Mariners who sailed their own schooners on trading voyages as far as the Black Sea. In the small graveyard in Mornington at the mouth of the river Boyne, there is a headstone over the Boylan family grave. It records the death in 1879 of my grandfather Captain William Boylan, who was the last of the family to own and sail his own schooner, the 84 ton *Eagle,* a vessel close in size to the present sail-training brigantine

Asgard II. Family legend recalls that his voyages took him along the coast of France and Spain, into the Mediterranean and through the Sea of Marmara as far as Constantinople (now Istanbul), returning with silks and spices from the East. On his passage home he would put into ports in Spain and France for wines and brandy. There was a ready market for these wares from prosperous merchants in Drogheda and the landed gentry who were still living very well in their 'Big Houses' in the surrounding rich lands of Meath and Louth.

However, the same family lore relates his relatively early death. It seems that on the passage home in 1879, my grandfather put into Bordeaux for wine. Coming back aboard carrying presents for the family he slipped on the deck and injured himself. He took to his bunk and died before reaching Drogheda. His death was probably due to his hitting his head on the deck or on an iron stanchion. He was then in his mid-forties and left a young widow with two children, my father, then in his early teens and his young sister. The widow was obliged to sell the *Eagle* and that was the end of 'the Boylan line'.

In the family tradition, my father followed the sea, but as there was now no family schooner for him to take over, at sixteen he shipped in Liverpool on the *Dun Cow*, a three-masted tea-clipper. Those were the days of 'wooden ships and iron men', and one had to be strong, active, hardy and fearless to serve on those windjammers. Whatever the weather, hail, rain or snow, sails had to be set or furled, men had to go aloft and lay out along the yards, 'one hand for yourself and one for the owner'. It was dangerous work; many a sailor fell to his death when handing sail with the wind blowing a gale and the sail threshing like a mad thing.

A photograph taken in San Francisco in the 1890s shows my father and crew aboard ship in harbour. He had qualified as Master Mariner when he was only twenty-seven. Officers and crew in the Merchant Service did not wear a uniform at that time, and referred to the Royal Navy scornfully as 'brass bound lounge lizards'. In this photograph his position shows that he was Captain. The crew always spoke of the Captain as 'the old man', be he twenty-one or fifty. My father told me of an encounter with one of the notorious 'boarding house crimps' on his first visit to San Francisco ten years earlier. American Captains and their 'bucko' mates had a fearsome reputation for their brutal 'discipline' and no sailor would willingly sign on with them. The crimp came on board as soon as a ship berthed. 'I have a great job waiting for you,' he told my father. 'Good pay and your boots under the bed every night.' My father had been warned and turned the offer down but some of his shipmates, weary after long months at sea, could not resist. In the boarding house they were plied with drugged drink and woke up twenty-four hours later on board a Yankee clipper, well out to sea, shanghaied by the crimp who was paid by the Captain for every man he delivered on the eve of sailing.

Conditions were hard. My father once told how on a voyage to Australia the mate was struck by an excruciating toothache while they were thousands of miles from the nearest port and had no doctor aboard. Nearly driven mad by the pain, he resorted to an heroically extreme measure, and reddening a needle in the galley fire, he cauterised the offending tooth.

Faced with tough men, the officers had to be tough themselves. If any of the men got abusive and truculent with the ship hundreds or thousands of miles from port, with no police there to call on, the Captains had to deal with the malcontents themselves. Their strong personalities and habit of command usually won the day, but if the trouble persisted, boot and fist came into play and were used freely.

Father spoke caustically about a certain Captain K, a small man, still, a qualified Master Mariner. 'What does he mean, calling himself Captain? He never had a command. Who would put him over a crew? He's too small, he wouldn't be able to discipline them.' Even in later years my father had a hand gun, licensed of course, which I saw by accident in a drawer, on the *Mellifont* his second command, but this was a really last resort and he never had to produce it. At a broad-shouldered five foot ten, with a stentorian voice, this and his reputation as a former tea-clipper mate, made him a formidable figure, not to be crossed lightly.

Having sailed the seven seas and seen the world, my father took time off to attend nautical school, qualified as Master Mariner, and joined the Drogheda Steam Packet Co., which had been founded in 1826. Home again, in 1900 he married Mary Coleman and settled down, becoming Master of the paddle steamer *Norah Creina* (the 'wise and prudent Norah') and then of the twin-screw *Mellifont*, operating a passenger and cargo service between Drogheda and Liverpool three times a week. The service was popular in those days with local merchants and the landed gentry. They could go on board at Drogheda, have a good meal and sleep in a comfortable cabin for the rest of the ten-hour passage to Liverpool. And even if the *Mellifont* had to sail early to catch the tide, the passengers could stay on board in Liverpool to a reasonable hour.

The *Mellifont*, built in 1903, was accounted a fine up-to-date ship, with good passenger accommodation, but like all ships at the time, had an open bridge, so that officers and men on watch had little protection from the weather. On a bad winter's night, crossing the bar, my father told me, she would roll until her bridge went right under and filled with the icy water of the Boyne, the men on watch standing in it nearly up to their shoulders. It would take over an hour before the ship was safely berthed above the Viaduct and the soaked crew could change to dry clothing.

There was a brisk trade with England in live cattle and sheep. As the song had it:

> *Sure the best of Welsh mutton and English roast beef,*
> *Came over in ships from old Ireland.*

The cattle dealers, big, stout, red-faced men in frieze overcoats, embarked with their charges and the drovers, who spent the passage in the cargo hold, tending to the cattle and sheep. The dealers stayed up all night drinking and playing poker in the saloon. The bar attendants spoke with awe of the thick wads of bank notes flung across the tables. On rough passages they would occasionally slip down to the hold to check on their terrified beasts. The cargo was unloaded at Birkenhead and the dealers went ashore to the markets. Late that evening they would straggle back on board, having been on their feet all day bargaining, arguing and drinking. But now they would make straight for their bunks and spend the passage back to Drogheda sleeping like the dead.

My father said that crossing the Irish Sea he had met weather as bad as any he had encountered in the Atlantic or Pacific. 'One night with a head wind of strong gale force, we were abreast of a light for three hours under full steam ahead but unable to make any headway in the violent sea. Her bow would rise up and up, then plunge down again and her stern would come clean out of the water, the twin screws racing madly, and she would shake from stem to stern as if in the grip of a giant hand.' From one of the crew, I heard of another such night, when the *Mellifont* plunged from the crest of a thirty-foot sea into a threatening dark abyss. The terrified helmsman abandoned the wheel but was met by by 'the old man' with a fearful clout to the head and a stern order 'Get back to your wheel'.

Fog was the worst feared hazard. He recalled how one night 'a thick fog came down as we were coming into the fairway to Liverpool port. We could hear the foghorns of the ships moored ahead of us on each side of the fairway, bleating away like frightened sheep, their anchors down as they feared to stir in the fog. It lifted a bit then and I darted her forward a couple of cable lengths until the fog closed down again. Down anchor and wait, then another lift of the fog and full ahead again and in this way I made it to the Collingwood Dock. We were the only steamer to dock that night,' said he.

It is a traditional shipboard custom that distinguished passengers are invited to dine at the Captain's table. In this way, my father got to know quite a few of the local gentry and merchants, and he told me of a local landowner, a gentleman jockey, crossing to Liverpool where he had a mount in the Grand National. He was seriously injured in a bad fall at Becher's Brook and on arrival back at Drogheda he was taken off the *Mellifont* on a stretcher 'with every bone in his body broken', according to the vivid account current in the town. Nothing daunted, the following year with his bones apparently set again, he rode in the Grand National and got round safely on this second attempt.

The First World War brought a new hazard to the passage to Liverpool, especially from February 1917 when the Germans initiated an intense U-boat blockade. The danger was very real—over 150 vessels were sunk in a single four-week period. Once the more or less defenceless merchant ship was spotted, torpedoes would blow a huge hole in a ship's side and send her to the bottom in anything from two to seven minutes. Essential imports, such as coal, began to run short. But also the Germans were well aware that thousands of Irishmen had volunteered for service in the British Forces and that they returned to Ireland on leave from time to time. The most famous sinking was that of the mailboat *Leinster*, carrying hundreds of such soldiers. It was torpedoed in October 1918 near the Kish Lightship in Dublin Bay and sank in seven minutes. Five hundred and one lives were lost and 256 survivors rescued by British destroyers.

It must have been during those years that my father began his habit of kissing good-bye to all the family as he left to board the *Mellifont* and sail to Liverpool in the darkened ship. Several of his junior officers were unable to endure the strain and left to find jobs ashore, on farms or behind shop counters, anything rather than the sea. One of them refused to go below when off duty and slept on deck so that if the *Mellifont* was torpedoed he would not be trapped below.

I was too young to understand the strain of those years on my father and mother and it was only in later years (during the Second World War) when brother Willy had several narrow escapes that my father told me of the effects of the danger on some of his young officers. Fortunately, the *Mellifont* survived.

'Baldy' Reynolds, a river pilot on the Boyne, was one of the local characters. There were so many Reynolds in Mornington that many had distinguishing nicknames, 'The Dasher', 'The Brother', 'The Cobra', 'John the Neighbour', 'Peter the Block', etc. Baldy had lost all his hair in his early teens and was promptly given his nickname in the insensitive fashion of the times. It was said that at Mass one Sunday as a boy, he was soundly slapped on his bald head by a short-sighted woman in the seat behind him, who hissed at him, 'Turn round to the altar and stop staring at me, you impudent brat.' I got to know him in the summer holidays from school when I used to go swimming at his native village, Mornington, at the mouth of the river on the south side. He was then a stocky weather-beaten man of indeterminate age.

The bar at the mouth of the Boyne is dangerous in bad weather and navigable for steamers only at high tide, so the ships crossed the bar when the tide suited which could be two in the morning or ten at night. My father was a qualified pilot, and knew the Boyne well, but visiting vessels needed the services of a local pilot to guide them in. Pilots would watch out for these vessels and then race each other, competing to be first to set foot on the ship and gain the job. This system ended when a pilot lost his footing, fell into the sea and drowned.

Besides piloting, Baldy worked for my father's shipping company., always on hand to help with docking and casting off. He would put out from Mornington in his 18-foot sailing yawl and range alongside the steamer when it had crossed the bar. A tow rope was thrown down to him and he was towed the three miles to the quays at

Drogheda. There he would cast off the tow and scull to the quay, scrambling up to catch the mooring hawsers from the ship and loop them over the bollards on the quay. When the ship sailed on the next tide, Baldy was at hand, skipping nimbly about the quay to let go the mooorings. He then jumped into his yawl and was towed down river, casting off at Mornington and sculling in to the landing place near his cottage. I watched him many times come tearing down the river astern of the steamer and then scull sedately to where I sat on the river bank, sunning myself after a swim.

One day as he was busy casting off the mooring hawsers on the quay near our house, I said to him impulsively 'I'd love to make a trip down river with you.' 'Well, come on, then,' and he led the way down slippery steps to where his boat nudged the quay wall.

I followed down and sat in the stern. He hailed the ship—it was the *Mellifont*—and a tow-rope came whistling down. He made it fast to the forward thwart or seat. I saw with some astonishment that he made several turns of the tow-rope round the seat, which was a stout plank a good inch-and-a-half thick, jointed into even stouter ribs and secured by strong 'knees'. He shipped a steering oar over the stern and we moved off in the wake of the steamer. Holding the oar firmly in his great, hairy fist, Baldy steered his yawl at an angle from the ship, so that we slipped along slightly ahead of her propellers. As the *Mellifont* gathered speed, the tow-rope began to make a sort of groaning noise, and the seat groaned in reply. The bow of the yawl began to rise up and the water foamed away each side. As the ship increased speed, the bow lifted higher, and the seat started to shake and gave out a continuous groan. The whole boat was like a live thing, fighting against the wave streaming past. Now I knew that an 18-foot yawl could not be driven through the water under sail at more than 6 knots, no matter what sail she carried. Naval architects have a formula for maximum speed, based on the length of a boat on the waterline. The yawl was being hauled through and over the waves at about 8 knots, well above her maximum sailing speed. Now I realised why Baldy had wound the tow-rope round the seat. An ordinary fitting would have been pulled out in a minute.

On we tore, from time to time the bow hit a wave and the yawl bounced up and banged down again, throwing a sheet of spray over us. He now had the steering oar cradled under his left arm with his right hand gripping its end. I noticed for the first time that he had a hatchet handy on the floor boards. I did not need to be told that it was there to sever the tow-rope in an emergency. I tingled with excitement and some fear and assured myself that if we capsized, I was a good enough swimmer to make it to the river bank. I wondered could Baldy swim? Probably not, his generation had a fatalistic attitude to drowning. I threw an apprehensive look at the propellers. Would they suck you in and mash you to pieces? I was only thirteen, too young to die. Just then, Baldy muttered something to himself and I saw that he was staring at the bridge of the *Mellifont*. I looked up and saw a familiar-looking burly figure watching us. The watcher put his binoculars to his eyes. 'Holy God, it's your old man,' said Baldy. The man on the bridge resumed his walk up and down, pausing to throw a swift look down at us from time to time. 'Did he know you were coming with me?' I shook my head and he muttered a curse. Our bow was now several feet higher than the stern, the tow-rope and seat gave out a continuous groaning, drumming sound, the wind whistled in my ears and the bow wave added its voice to the uproar. We went on at this headlong speed for what seemed a long time but it cannot have been more than about twenty minutes when we came abreast of Mornington.

A sailor signalled to Baldy and then cast off the tow-rope. The yawl slackened speed miraculously, and Baldy sculled furiously to take us away from the thrashing propellers. In ten minutes I was sitting in his cottage, while his wife fussed around, scolding Himself for letting me get wet and preparing a cup of scalding tea.

My father did not return for three days but he had not forgotten. Fixing me with his piercing gaze, like a veritable Ancient Mariner, he said, 'Don't let me catch you again, towing with that ruffian, Reynolds.'

I met Baldy for the last time on a visit to Drogheda some forty years later. He nearly knocked me down, rounding a corner on a blowy day, muffled in his old reefer jacket. He was hurrying back to Mornington to pilot a ship upriver. He must have been then near to eighty.

Docking in Drogheda required good seamanship and it was a treat to see my father 'swinging' the *Mellifont*, which was nearly the full width of the river at full tide. It required skill and a nice touch with both helm and engines to carry out the manoeuvre successfully. He would steer the *Mellifont* almost but not quite into the soft mud on the Meath side, just above the Viaduct, and as the flood tide swung her stern around, it was slow astern on her engines and she would back gently across to her berth. It was only too easy to get her bow stuck in the mud and then to go astern too hard in the effort to extricate the vessel, which would tend to come back across to the quay wall at terrifying speed. Dockside loafers and longshoremen were connoisseurs of this free spectacle.

The misfortunate experience of one Captain was retold with relish over many a pint. By misjudgement, he had got his ship stuck in the mud. There was great shouting of advice from the quayside, a boat set out and took a line ashore with a hawser attached. Willing hands hauled it to a bollard, dropped the loop over and the shout went up, 'Heave away'. But the ship's crew hove too heartily on the capstan, the hawser tightened, sprang out of the water and the ship came out of the mud like a cork out of a bottle. The vessel charged down on the quay and her counter swept away ten yards of railing and a watchman's hut. A heaving line was thrown from her bows but fell short. Another boat put off, retrieved the line and got it ashore. It is far from easy to control several thousand tons of ship on a flood tide in a narrow channel and a full hour of drama followed before the vessel was safely moored alongside, with her Captain and the Harbour Master gloomily contemplating the damage done to ship and quay works.

If a ship was too late for the tide and could not swing, she had to berth alongside the quay with her bow facing upstream. This gave rise to a local saying, 'Were you in time for Mass/the concert/the match? Barely. I just got in bow-up.' Joseph Conrad, no doubt, had greater catastrophes in mind, but still, his words echo in my mind. He wrote, 'Of all the living creatures upon land and sea, it is ships that cannot be taken in by barren pretences, that will not put up with bad work from their masters.'

The shipping company my father worked for was taken over by the LMS Railway Company. Railway companies were then regarded as good employers, almost on a level with banks and Guinness and especially valued for their pension plans. He retired about 1927 when I was fifteen and I got to know him a lot better. Previously, his appearances at home were limited to two or three days in the week and the time of his arrival varied with the tide. If the *Mellifont* berthed in the early morning, he would have spent the night on watch on the bridge. He would come home, a five-minute walk with the ship's boy to carry his bag, in time for breakfast *en famille* and retire to bed to catch up on his sleep. He would be at home for a few hours in the evening before going on board late at night to take command for a sailing in the small hours. Other days time and tide dictated that his time at home was cut even shorter.

Father had the sight of an eagle, even in his late seventies. I was with him one day on Donors Green, watching a rare visitor, a three-masted sailing ship, down river making for the bar. She was nearly three miles distant and though I had good long sight, I could barely make her out. He said suddenly, 'She's gone aground.' He continued to watch intently, then, 'She's off again.' I could see no movement. That evening I met her pilot. 'Yes, she took the ground for a couple of minutes, just past Mornington'. (In the early nineteenth century, people with weak eyesight were often advised by their doctor to take a long sea voyage. One such was Richard Henry Dana, a young law student from Boston, author of that classic of life aboard a sailing ship, *Two Years Before the Mast* (1840). With his sight permanently cured, Dana pursued a career as barrister and politician and was disappointed at his very moderate success. In later years he remarked ruefully that such distinctions as he gained were an anti-climax to his 'great success, my book, my boy's work'.) As well as this, Father remained fit—in his seventies he would terrify the whole family by climbing to the very top of our huge old apple tree—delicious 'Blood of the Boyne' variety—to collect the ripe fruit.

The Master of a ship is accountable for everything that happens on his ship, whether he himself is present or not, and one afternoon we had a vivid lesson in how seriously my father took this responsibility. Two sailors arrived at our front door, looking very worried and asked to see Father. After a short exchange he came back into the house with a face like thunder, put on his uniform cap and went off with them. He was back within the hour to collect his gear as the *Mellifont* was due to sail. Afterwards we learned what had happened. The young Third Officer had ordered one of the sailors to hoist the Blue Peter, a flag signalling that the ship would sail shortly and warning all concerned to report on board. The halyards got entangled near the top of the mast and the officer ordered the sailor to go aloft and free the flag. The sailor was a middle-aged man who probably had not been aloft for years. He lost his grip and foothold, fell forty feet to the deck and was killed instantly. He should never have been sent aloft. One of the young men should have been sent in his place.

I had never seen my father look so upset. The dead man had sailed with him for over twenty years and my father liked and respected him as a loyal and capable sailor. That unnecessary death of an old friend and shipmate affected him deeply.

My father had a good baritone voice and I regret that I did not write down some of his songs of the sea. I have not been able to trace them in any published collections. But I do remember one nonsense song:

> *Haylee go maylee go, lay me down dee,*
> *Lay me down itchy back, Mrs Mackay,*
> *Mrs Mahoolego, jinny ma hoo,*
> *Fire away ladder, I'm dying for you.*

Rattled out *con brio*, I've used it very occasionally to dodge coaxing for a 'party piece'.

2 Willy

We called him Willy. Born in about 1900, he was the eldest boy of the family of nine and eleven years older than me. My first recollection is of mother saying 'Any divilment there was in the town, Willy Boylan was blamed for it.' He had in full measure the energy of most boys of that age, which had to find an outlet some way. There was little by way of pastime available to them, no organised games or clubs. The ways they adopted to amuse themselves and pass the time had no tinge of real harm or evil—they did not break into houses or steal and I never heard that they ever threatened elderly people. Robbing orchards was a favourite diversion. With his following of half-a-dozen like-minded lads— he was always the leader—he would sally out a mile or so into the country where they knew the best orchards and the temper of the various owners. What they objected to most was not the loss of a couple of dozen of apples or pears, but the damage done to the trees, fences and walls. Branches were sometimes broken when boys used their full weight to pull them down to reach the biggest and ripest of the fruit. Gaps were unheedingly made in walls and hedges and could allow stray cattle to get in and do further damage. So the owners kept a watch out for raiding boys and this added a spice of danger as they would suddenly appear, shouting, cursing, brandishing horse whips and setting their dogs on the marauders.

Strangely enough, my mother told me that when Willy was only about seven years old, he was terrified of feathers. To keep him at home, all she had to do was to send him upstairs on some pretext and place a feather half-way. She could be assured that he would not come down past the feather. A few years later it would take more than a feather to spancel him.

Willy was always mitching from school and as my father's visits home twice a week did not last more than effectively a very few hours, my mother had to try to impose some discipline herself. By this time the family had grown to six and she had her hands full. So Willy was a real problem. He solved the problem by running away to sea when he was thirteen. When he was fourteen, he signed on in Liverpool as A.B. (able-bodied) seaman on a three-masted, square-rigged tea clipper bound for China. Years later when my father told me this, I said, 'An A.B.? But he was only fourteen, a schoolboy.'

'Yes, but he was as big and strong as a man.'

The family lost sight and track of him for long intervals but he always signalled his visits home by banging the front door knocker so vigorously that it came clean off. So when we came home from school and saw that the knocker was gone, Willy was home for another short visit. He was still restless, and after a few voyages to China and Japan, he shipped on a vessel bound for Canada. He jumped ship in Quebec and went lumber-jacking for a season. He then made his way to New York, where an uncle had a small printing house and stayed working with him for six months before taking to the sea again.

My mother more than once said to me how glad she was that Willy was at sea in the years following the Rising of Easter Week 1916. She was quite certain that had he been in Ireland during the War of Independence he would have joined the Volunteers. 'He would have been in the thick of it,' she would say, leaving unsaid the dread that he would be shot dead in an ambush or other encounter with the Black and Tans or the Auxiliaries.

Next I heard that, after four or five years of this life, he had enrolled at a Nautical College in Liverpool and was studying to qualify as an officer and, hopefully, as Master Mariner. His formal education was virtually non-existent but he had a naturally quick mind. I think it must have been my father's saying to him, 'You don't want to spend the rest of your life as an Ordinary Seaman,' or perhaps he had come to the same conclusion himself and it needed just the 'push' from Father to take action. He came home a few times in the College vacations and we had sessions together in the back garden, practising taking sights with a sextant, still in use then for determining a ship's position by its latitude and longitude at noon by the chronometer. I was able to help him with the elements of Geometry also required for navigation. He was well-versed in practical seamanship, ship handling in bad weather, the care of sails and rigging and had learned quite a lot about ship engines, capstans, donkey engines and other engineering equipment, having been taken in hand by the Chief Engineer of the *Mellifont*, who knew that my father would be pleased by this attention. I said to Willy one day, 'You wouldn't want all this, especially the navigation, just for crossing to Liverpool or any English port or skippering a fishing trawler.' He gave me a look that reminded me of my father's piercing gaze and said, 'The old man would throw me out if I came home with just a miserable Coasting Ticket.' Today's technology using satellites has produced the capacity to determine a ship's position to within a matter of yards. Sextant and chronometer are gone and the use of the system and equipment is easily mastered.

Willy went on to qualify as Master Mariner. Father was quite upset when steamship services from the Irish coast to British ports were amalgamated as Coast Lines Ltd, in the 1920s. 'Take your brother Willy,' he said. Willy had not yet been appointed to a command. 'If he finds himself serving as Chief Officer under some cranky tyrant of a skipper, before this he could give the brute a puck in the lug, sling his hook and he'd have a choice of half-a-dozen companies. Now they are all the one,' shaking his head gloomily.

However, Willy got command within a month and the crisis passed.

Willie was tough. On one occasion a particularly Bolshie seaman refused to do what he was told, and told Willy what he thought of him, ending with a recommendation that he should f— off! Willy, forgetting he was on the quays in Drogheda and not at sea, let fly with an uppercut that laid the seaman out. This was a sackable offence in the eyes of the union, but luckily another sailor had the wit to fetch my father from Riverside only a few minutes away. The offender turned out to be a distant relative, a Reynolds from Mornington, and my father, with some trouble persuaded him to drop any complaint. As it happened the sailor had no support from the rest of the crew ('Reynolds had it coming to him') who rather admired their Captain's toughness.

After a few years 'foreign-going' as the sailors called it, Willie joined the British and Irish Steamship Company and in due course was appointed to a command. He married and settled in Liverpool, the terminus for B & I services from Dublin and Drogheda. Crossing the Irish Sea one night with him, I saw he had posted a sailor at the end of the bridge, outside the wheel-house.

'Why have you that poor devil out there in the cold and rain?' I asked.

'Because he'll see more and better,' was the short answer.

'But you have a radar screen in the wheel-house!'

'The radar can break down.'

There was no answer to that.

In Liverpool he was required to moor his ship in the Gladstone Dock. Manoeuvring in and out of dock was far from easy as there was only a foot or so to spare on each side. Many Captains made very heavy weather of this operation, backing and filling, with hawsers out fore and aft and men on the dock wall with fenders at the ready. With Willy it was 'Slow ahead, slow astern, ahead and out.' The engineers watching the telegraph conveying orders from the bridge would say 'We have "old three moves" up there tonight.'

The outbreak of the Second World War brought the same danger of attacks by U-boats in the Irish Sea as in the First World War. Willy had some narrow escapes. He was assigned to the SS *Ardmore* but at the last moment he was put in charge of the MV *Inisfallen*. The *Ardmore* sailed from Liverpool without him. She was never heard of again. In 1940 he was in command of the *Inisfallen* when she was sunk by mines off New Brighton. All of the passengers were saved but four crew members lost their lives. Nineteen forty-two saw his most dangerous involvement in the war when he volunteered to take part in a convoy from the USA.

The Battle of the Atlantic was then at its height. Germany sought to bring about the total blockade of Britain, to deprive her of vital supplies of food and oil and to foil any invasion of Europe by sinking ships carrying armed forces and military equipment. In 1942 their U-boats sank 1,000 ships in convoy to Britain, a loss of over 5 million tons. Nevertheless the same year 226,000 Allied fighting men arrived in Britain. The 'monster liners' *Queen Mary* and *Queen Elizabeth* carried 15,000 troops each and others carried from 4,500 to 8,000. These great ships sailed singly and their high speed and the total secrecy of their routes and sailings enabled them to evade the U-boats. The smaller merchant cargo-carrying vessels bore the brunt of attacks by the U-boat Wolf Packs, hence the enormous losses in 1942. In addition, the Luftwaffe attacked Britain's dockyards and ports resulting in a shortfall of one million tons between merchant ships lost and new ships being built. On the other hand heavy bombing of Germany by the Allied Air Forces resulted in great losses of bombers and crews but the numbers of U-boats built and commissioned was unaffected. It was generally believed that Air Chief Marshal 'Bomber' Harris was convinced that bombing alone would force Germany into surrender, without invasion, but German factories, if anything, increased production after this intensive bombing. The situation in the North Atlantic was vitally affected by Harris's decision to divert long-range bombers to the attacks on Germany, thus leaving a gap of 300 square miles in the North Atlantic without air cover. The gap became known as the Black Pit and allowed the U-boats to concentrate their patrols and Wolf Packs there, immune to attacks from coastal command aircraft.

Planning for an invasion of Europe after the USA had entered the War, the Allies needed to provide ships for hospital and cross-channel personnel. The USA offered lake excursion ships which had been popular with honeymoon couples so the Americans christened the convoy 'the Honeymoon Fleet.' The Allies had to provide the crews to sail them to England, and Coast Lines, incorporating the B & I, undertook to find volunteers for this dangerous mission and Willy was amongst them. The crews, numbering 550 officers and men, sailed to New York in the *Queen Mary* and on 21 September 1942 the fleet of eight lake ships and two escorting destroyers sailed from St Johns, Newfoundland. Willy was Captain of the SS *Yorktown*.

There were many strange aspects of this convoy, giving rise to questions as to its real purpose. The ships themselves, lake pleasure steamers, were never intended for crossings of the North Atlantic. When five of them eventually reached the UK, there were difficulties in finding suitable roles for them. The ships were strengthened and boarded up heavily and had guns installed. They sailed with the season of equinoctial gales not far ahead and were escorted by two of the oldest destroyers in the Royal Navy, which were unable to steam at high speeds or carry on continuous attacks on U-boats.

The convoy was given an official code name, 'Maniac'. Captain J. Beckett, Master of the *Northland*, one of the ships which escaped the U-boats, observed sarcastically that the code name was very appropriate, but should have been in the plural. The profile of the ships, with their high superstructure and high funnels, seems to have misled the U-boat command which reported sighting an

A Voyage Round My Life

important convoy of large troop transports, including ships of the *Queen Mary* class, and their high command considered it so important that they ordered 17 U-boats to move to attack. After three unsuccessful attempts, they torpedoed and sank three ships and one of the escorting destroyers, all putting up strong resistance with gunfire and depth charges. Berlin radio claimed the action as a great success in destroying a large troopship convoy despite a fierce defence. Willy's ship the SS *Yorktown* was one of those sunk; 302 men in all lost their lives. Willy survived. An article by him, published in *Sea Breezes*, follows.

Loss of the Yorktown
By Capt. W. P. Boylan

We sailed from St. John N. F. on September 21, 1942, for the United Kingdom, in convoy. Three days later the escort informed us that we were being shadowed by enemy submarines and to expect attack that night; Watches were doubled now and strict blackout enforced, but no attack took place that night. About 2 p.m. on September 25, the commodore ship, with Capt. Young in charge, received two torpedoes on the starboard side and as we watched two torpedoes were seen coming towards us. We avoided these by helm action and all ships opened out to let the escort come in to attack, the submarine being in the middle of the convoy.

About 4 p.m. the convoy was reformed under Capt. Mayers (Vice-Commodore) and we proceeded on zigzag course. About 6 p.m. Capt. Mayers informed us that surface raiders were in the vicinity and to keep a sharp look-out.

About 8 p.m. we found that the ship was not steering too good, and investigation showed the wires around the engine to be tangled up and both wires going the same way. I at once reported to Capt. Mayers and told him I would drop out to remedy the matter. Engines were stopped and taking all hands on watch except the second officer and fourth engineer we set about disconnecting the wires from the barrel. We had got well on with the job when there was a violent explosion, the ship rattled and shuddered and everyone hung on to something; the bosun very laconically remarked "Depth

[20]

charges" so all set to work again.

About 10 or 15 seconds later a similar explosion took place, the bosun again remarked "Depth charges," but I decided to get up on top and see what was happening.

On arrival at the bridge the second officer reported nothing wrong with us, but drew my attention to the convoy now on the horizon sending up snowflakes in bunches, flashes from gun-fire and concussion from torpedoes or depth charges. It seemed as if the convoy was getting wiped out.

I advanced the theory that the two explosions were from torpedoes fired at us but outrun their distance (this I may add was also the theory of the Casualty Section, Whitehall).

About 10 p.m. the steering gear was reported serviceable and course was set at right angles to the convoy track to get away if possible from the U-boat pack. At 12 p.m. course was set for the channel. The weather was now strong westerly wind with rough sea, drizzling rain and poor visibility.

The night and following day passed without any further incident except that owing to the heavy sea it was impossible to zigzag.

At 8 p.m. September 26 the second officer and I turned the watch over to the chief and third officer, and hopes were now high as we were only about 300 miles from Tory Island and enemy submarines had long ago decided that this vicinity was not too healthy for them. However, about 9 p.m. there was an awful crash and I found myself and the bunk falling through space with various kinds of debris on top of me. Coming to rest in pitch darkness, no torch even available and the ship just wallowing and more debris crashing with every surge.

I realised coolness was essential, so listening carefully for something, anything just to get an idea where I was and how best to get out of it, I heard sounds which suggested at least open air and made a scramble in that direction, pulling, pushing, crawling under and over debris. Stopping again I could now hear water lapping, and, scrambling away again finally arrived out at the ship's side or at least where the ship's side had been.

Standing knee deep in water and looking around, I saw utter desolation. The funnel and two gun turrets were directly over me and looking forward all that was now visible was the D.F. loop just over the water.

There was a considerable amount of surging underneath me and a heavy snapping crack (which I took to be No. 2 bulkhead giving out) and the ship began to sink. I took to the water hoping for the best as she was going quickly and appeared to list towards me, which made me get a move on. However, she straightened up and rose perpendicular as she went with the steam whistle going full blast.

I now came across a door, and half lying on it managed to get some of my wind back. Catching the door by the sides I was raising myself up to see what was around when the door cracked in the middle and both parts hit me in the face so I promptly let go and fell between them. Striking out again I got hold of some more wreckage and held on.

A heavy sea was running, weather was misty but the moon gave a little light; little red lights bobbed here and there; one or two white raft flares showed heaps of wreckage grinded together and men clung to it shouting, and some actually singing, and other cries as if from birds. The I spotted a raft about 200 yards away and decided that was my only hope so struck out for it at once. I finally made it and was hauled on board by the chief engineer and a fireman, the only occupants.

It took me some time to recover.

We searched amongst the big wreckage and picked up men here and there, the last being the second warrant officer; it was a job to locate him, sometimes we could hear a faint cry and then not a sound, but we traced him. He made the number up to nineteen and a very fine crowd of men they were, most helpful, cheerful and unselfish.

Next afternoon (September 27) a four-engined bomber spotted us and coming down almost to sea level circled round and round. It was given a hearty wave each time which was willingly returned and all hands cheered. The plane stayed with us for about two hours and before going away dropped a bag of provisions, etc., quite close, but unfortunately the raft was too heavily laden and unwieldy to get near.

However, nobody worried much now knowing we would be reported at once. I told the men not to expect anything for 24 hours, due to the weather and we bedded down for the night after having our allowances of chocolate, biscuits and a double ration of water as a celebration.

I have heard many stories about seamen's boarding houses, but they had nothing on us that night. Finding your own legs if you wanted to move or turn was a hopeless job and caused many a laugh, many after massaging a leg for five or ten minutes found it to be someone else's.

Next morning (Monday September 28) an old negro fireman was found dead and after searching him for any documents he was buried.

The raft by this time was beginning to show signs of her heavy cargo and we packed all the lifebelts into the body to help her and try to keep us from lying in the water.

About 1 p.m. smoke was seen on the horizon; it was most anxiously watched and later identified as a destroyer. Everybody now became cheerful and jokes were passed. We watched the destroyer pick up the lifeboats and also the chief officer's raft and then she steamed away, passing us about a mile away. We had a small flag on a paddle and we shouted and whistled but on she went and passed out of sight over the horizon.

That was heartbreaking indeed, but to the credit of everyone I never heard one wrong expression of criticism or pessimism.

Time wore on and as twilight set in I began to feel very doubtful and finally decided we might as well have our rations, bed down, and hope for the best at daylight. It was now almost dark and nearly all hands half asleep when there was a yell from the second warrant officer "There's the destroyer," and sure enough there she was about a mile away passing the other side now. Getting the torch and with a couple holding me up I flashed away and all hands shouted. It was a relief to see his lights alter and he bore straight down on us.

Inside ten minutes we were all safely on board where we received the utmost hospitality and kindness.

Incidentally, the captain of the destroyer informed me that we were very lucky indeed as our raft was level with the water and would be very hard to see unless quite close.

All hands were landed in Derry. Seventeen were taken to hospital suffering from exposure, but a couple of days put all hands well enough to travel home.

In *Convoy Maniac* (2000), Jim Reid, a gunner on the escorting destroyer *Vanoc* which survived the crossing, quotes from articles stating that 'Maniac' was in fact a decoy convoy, intended to draw the U-boats from attacking a very large munitions and troopship convoy which sailed from America at the same time and got through safely.

Like many episodes of the war, the whole truth about this convoy may remain for ever clouded in uncertainty and doubts. Clandestine operations, decoys and false information were freely used in desperate situations. Jim Reid outlined the pressures on the two sides:

> The Battle of the Atlantic was a sea war that had no equal in history. For almost six years it was a cruel and savage war of attrition, in thousands of square miles of ocean, in most appalling weather, ferocious gales and low temperatures. The object of this maritime slaughter of human beings and sinking of ships was:
>
> For the Allies: to preserve the vital supply life-line from the American and Canadian seaboard across the Atlantic to the United Kingdom, a task that must not fail as the future of the whole free world depended on it. Without food supplies Britain would face starvation and defeat. Without armed forces and supplies coming over to the UK there could be no invasion of Europe. A total blockade of Britain would have resulted in capitulation.
>
> For the Germans: The total blockade of Britain, making it impossible for it to survive or retaliate. The losses to the Allies ran into millions of tons of shipping and thousands of lives. The German Navy lost over 1000 U-boats and 70% of their crews. The victory they sought was at times only a whisker away.

In *The Second World War*, vol v, p.6, Winston Churchill wrote:

> The battle of the Atlantic was the dominating factor all through the war. Never for one moment could we forget that everything happening elsewhere, on land, at sea, or in the air, depended ultimately on its outcome, and amid all other cares we viewed its changing fortunes day by day with hope or apprehension.

Willy was awarded the OBE in the next Honours List. His citation in the *London Gazette* reads, 'For outstanding courage and skilful seamanship during the passage of an important convoy which was subjected to heavy and sustained attacks by enemy submarines.' When asked why he, an Irishman, had volunteered for this dangerous mission he said simply 'I have earned my bread and butter in English ships all my life. I thought I owed them something.'

The Commanders of escorting destroyers get a clear view of the seamanship and leadership of the captains of the ships in the convoy. No doubt based on confidential reports, shortly after this award Willy was offered a commission with the Royal Navy as Commander, rising after a year to Captain, a rank equivalent to Colonel in the Army. It was a tempting offer since he was only forty-two years of age and entering at that seniority was virtually certain to reach the rank of Admiral. On the other hand his post in the B & I was exceptionally attractive for a Merchant Navy Captain as it ensured that he could see his wife and young family several times a week, whereas in the Royal Navy he would at best get home once a year for a few weeks and in wartime could not be certain of even this very limited contact. So he turned down the offer and went back to the Irish Sea route.

The strain of those war years and the long hours on watch and irregular meals had left Willy with digestive difficulties which he suspected might be due to ulcers. In 1960 he went into hospital in Liverpool for treatment and was told he had no ulcers but the surgeon decided to remove his appendix which he considered could give him trouble. Peritonitis developed and Willy died that night. He was only sixty. His death was classified as death by misadventure.

Willy's daughter Patricia had been a nurse before marrying a Syrian surgeon. She returned from her home in Damascus for the funeral and challenged the surgeon who had operated on Willy. He admitted he had been at fault, and Patricia wanted to sue, but Margaret (Cissie), Willy's widow, would not hear of it. As she said, 'it won't bring Willy back, and that's all I want.' She did not long survive him.

3 In Drogheda Town

I could not imagine how a boy could bear to live in a city, cut off from our daily pleasures on river and beach. Years later, I felt a flash of memory, hearing Breandán Ó hÉithir, the writer from Inishmore, tell a story about a boy of seventeen, Bartley, setting out from Aran to seek a job in Dublin. He hitched a lift as far as Kinnegad where he went into a small pub to ask for a bed for the night. The kindly owner and his wife gave him a good meal and put him up for the night. In the morning the man of the house said,

'Our pot-boy took himself off last week without saying a word to us. Would you like to stay and help us for a while?'

Bartley agreed straight away and all was fine until the next Friday when they said,

'You can have your half-day today.'

He took himself off and in an hour or so the wife called her husband,

'Johnny, Johnny, come up here till you see what Bartley is up to in the back field.'

He joined her at the top back window, looked out and saw Bartley climbing up a beech tree. When he was high up, he stood on a branch and holding on to a branch above, looked all around. Then he climbed down, ran over to another tree and climbed that one.

'Is the poor lad astray in the head?'

'Well, I'm after watching him this while and that's what he's doing all the time, running from one tree to the next and climbing up to look all round.'

Next morning there was another shock from Bartley.

'I'm very sorry, ma'am, but I have to go on.'

'Are we not treating you right, or what?'

'It's not that at all, ma'am, ye couldn't be nicer.'

'And what is it then, at all, at all?'

'Well, I'll tell you, ma'am, it's like this. I was reared to the sound of the sea and the sight of it, stretching away to the bottom of the sky, and I couldn't live without it. It would be too lonesome for an island boy.'

Then I remembered a story about another islander, Mick O'Connell, the famous footballer from Valentia Island. This was a good few years ago, before the bridge from Valentia to the mainland was built. It was often difficult, if not impossible, for Mick to get to Tralee for training sessions with the county team when the island was cut off in stormy weather. I was having a quiet drink one night in a pub in Cahirciveen and couldn't help overhearing the talk of a couple of Kerrymen nearby. They were talking football, what else and an All-Ireland Final coming up, with Kerry looking for another win?

Mick O'Connell was their hero and one of them spoke of the efforts of the County Board to make it easier for Mick to train with the team.

'They got a job for him in Tralee, but Mick couldn't settle into it anyway. He wasn't himself at all, on the field or off it.'

'And did he go back to the Island, then?'

'He did, indeed. He only stuck Tralee for a couple of weeks.'

'I'll tell you what, Mick do have a vocation for living on an island.'

As a boy growing up, I think I had a vocation for living on the banks of a river. When my father retired from the sea, he was elected a Harbour Commissioner and we had the use of a harbour boat, a strong rowing boat that could seat four, a safe, roomy craft. With my brothers or a school friend, I spent many hours rowing up and down the river. We thought nothing of rowing three miles to the mouth of the river, anchoring near the shore and wading to the beach to dig for sand eels for bait. Then row to a position just inside the bar, anchor again and start fishing for bass. With half a dozen two pounders in the bottom of the boat, we would head for home, sure of a welcome.

At that time the population of Drogheda was about 12,500, well below its post-Famine peak of 21,000, when the work was mostly in shipping and in linen. Unfortunately, the town was too small to compete in these industries with Belfast and Dublin, and the people migrated with the business. When I was a lad the only steady employment was provided by two linen mills, a flour mill and an oatmeal mill. There were, of course, the usual retailers and wholesalers who served the hinterland of comfortably-off farmers and Big Houses. The quay provided intermittent jobs loading and unloading ships. Working on the quays was hard and rough and the working conditions were primitive. Unloading a coal boat was one of the worst jobs. Half a dozen men were stationed in the hold, shovelling the coal into ten-stone bags. These were hoisted on deck by the ships' derricks, using rope slings. The men on deck lifted the bags on to their backs and ran down to the quay on a long gang-plank about two feet wide, bare of hand-rail, which bounced up and down with their weight. They ran across the quay to an open coal yard and emptied the bags there. It was dangerous and dirty work. The men in the hold were black with coal dust in a few hours. The men carrying the bags worked like coolies in the Far East; it was little better than slave labour.

The eldest in our family of nine was my sister May who was destined to become 'the girl who stayed at home', the one who was picked to help with a large family or an invalid mother, a familiar figure in those days. May was certainly very present in looking after us younger ones, helping with meals and so on. Mother (who had been born a Coleman) had a weak heart and retired to bed every afternoon to rest. I remember May rushing upstairs in a panic during one of her 'turns', clutching the brandy bottle. Later, May trained as a midwife, and set up a successful practice. Willy, the eldest boy, came next.

Then came Nan and Kitty who both came to Dublin and worked in the Civil Service and in Dublin Corporation before marrying and, as was the practice then, having to retire. Kitty wrote two well-received historical novels *Who Goes Home?* (1947) and *So Ends My Dream* (1950), which were republished in the 1980s. Her third son Ronan is at present Chief Justice. Her husband, John P. Keane, became Dublin City Manager. A dedicated racegoer, he later became Chairman of the unpaid Racing Board, which provides for the development of horse breeding and horse races and the better control of race courses.

My brother Jack, born in 1909, was the joker of the family. He was always in good humour, and in the close society of Drogheda he had the much appreciated skill of pinning down a neighbour's eccentricities with a telling phrase. 'What will we do for a laugh, Jack, when you're gone?' asked my mother when he left Drogheda for Dublin. He went to sea as a marine engineer, travelled the seven seas, and had his share of romancing the pretty daughters of cruise-goers, before marrying and settling in Dublin.

It is a sign of how few prospects there were in Drogheda if you hadn't family connections in some business that the next four children, Tom, myself, Una and the youngest, Joe, all came to Dublin and joined the public service. Tom worked in Dublin Corporation, Una, before marrying, worked for the Dublin Port and Docks Board, and Joe and I, the only ones still living, were in the Civil Service.

My maternal grandmother lived with us. She was a small, delicately-made woman, and to prove that she was not a burden, would insist on lifting heavy kettles full of water on to the kitchen range. My mother, rightly fearing that Granny would strain herself or let the kettle fall, would scold her and then Granny would say she was no use and no longer wanted. The next thing she would put on her hooded cloak, slip out and take away up the town and one of us would be dispatched to bring her back. Then there would be tears and recriminations on both sides and Granny would be re-assured that she was very much wanted and she would hug us all and be put to sit beside the fire in the most comfortable armchair in the house.

She must have lived into her late eighties, for I well remember her telling me of starving poor people coming to her family house in the famine years 1847/48 and seeing them ram the bread they were given into their mouths with their two hands.

Aunt Annie, my mother's sister, came every year to spend her holidays with us. She was a nun, a member of an order called, I think, the Daughters of the Heart of Mary. Her prayer books were all in French, so I thought that her order was French. Aunt Annie's personality is as vivid today, over fifty years later, as it was then. She was the most innocent person I ever knew, 'unacquainted with evil' and not capable of believing that anyone could do anything wrong deliberately. Quite probably she entered the order straight from school and had no experience whatever of the life led by people 'in the world'. On her visits with us she did not wear a nun's habit but dressed in black and would have passed as a widow.

In due course she became Mother Superior in her convent, with charge of an orphanage in Tivoli Road, Dún Laoghaire. Some of the boys were hard to control and one, called Tommy O'Reilly, was a real tearaway. He was always in trouble, but one day he excelled himself. In a violent outburst of manic energy he awarded a couple of black eyes to fellow orphans, broke several windows and kicked the shins of the Sisters who tried to restrain him. His conduct was so outrageous that it was reported to Mother Superior herself. Aunt

Annie sighed and said 'Poor Tommy, I'm afraid he has an innate lack of refinement.'

This was the strongest condemnation she could muster. The phrase passed into family folklore and whenever, for instance, a local blackguard broke loose and in a drunken row assaulted an innocent bystander, one of us was sure to say, ironically, 'So and so, the poor devil, he has an innate lack of refinement.'

Thanks to my father's job we were reasonably well-off, though with nine children there was no sense of luxury. We had a fine garden at the back of the house sloping up towards the next road with a row of loganberries, and five or six apple trees. The river was in front of the house. There was a narrow front garden facing south with a seat and he'd sit out there, chatting to passersby.

In the town, however, there was a dark side to life. Walking to school as a boy I saw something of the poverty of the people living in the back streets and lanes, some of whose houses were still roofed with thatch. Unemployed men, with nothing to do, would lean against the walls for hours—talking, playing cards, wasting away time. As an altar boy, one of my duties was to accompany the priest bringing Communion to the sick. One old woman lived alone in a one-roomed thatched cottage. She lay in a corner on a heap of rags. There was a fetid smell in the airless room and I could hardly get my breath for the few minutes we were there.

Quite a small increase in wages could make an enormous difference to lives in which opportunities were few. I remember Paddy Duffy, a hard-working man with a large family who worked in the Boyne Linen Mills for a miserable wage. He also got a small stipend as Assistant Secretary of the local GAA football club and for refereeing GAA matches, cycling miles in all weather to be there. Then the post of Secretary to the Drogheda Harbour Board came up, and my father, who was a Commissioner, decided to support Paddy's claim. We were living in Dublin at the time, so he took the train to Drogheda to attend the appointment meeting and I went with him. Paddy was a good candidate, and got the job which was secure, pensionable, came with a house and had good pay. When we went round to his house to give him the good news the poor man was overcome 'You're a Drogheda man,' he told my father, with tears running down his cheeks, 'and you've proved it today.'

Every weekday morning I was awakened at six by the women and girls clattering to work in the linen mills. At six in the evening they passed back, their talk tired and muted. They worked those hours six days a week and paid holidays were unknown. Our milk was delivered daily from a churn in a cart. Sometimes a small boy, son of the milkman, came with him to lead the horse. In winter the man's great hairy hands were red and purple with the cold. No wonder, he was wet through, with only an old sack thrown over his shoulders to ward off the sleet.

The great dread was tuberculosis, or consumption as it was called then. When a member of the well-off family of a prosperous merchant or the like, was found to have 'the consumption', he or she was often sent to a sanatorium in Switzerland for a year or longer. There the pure dry air, rest and skilled medical attention often effected a lasting cure. But the poor had no such care available to them and their standard of living left them with little or no defence against this modern plague. Long, dark winters, soakings in heavy rain, damp houses and deficient diets brought the inevitable result and TB seemed to single out some families through generations. I remember seeing two fine young women, sisters, going for a walk in Donors Green and my mother shaking her head in sorrow and saying, 'They have that high colour in their cheeks, a bad sign, I'm afraid they're not long for this world. It's in the family, God help them.' They died before the year was out and soon after we heard that their doctor, a new arrival in the town, had condemned their house on the quays as a death trap from its damp and warned the parents to leave it if they wanted to rear the rest of their young family.

The poor did not accept the miseries of their daily lives with resignation as 'the holy will of God'. The contrast with the comparative comfort enjoyed by the likes of clerks, tradesmen and small shopkeepers was resented. No, 'the will of God' was reserved for the misfortunes, illness and death, which befell rich and poor alike.

'Holy names' were freely used for emphasis in the conversation of the poor.

'Mother of God! You're wet through'.

'Oh, Sacred Heart! Did you ever hear the like!'

'Merciful hour! Would you look at the time!'

'Jesus, Mary and Joseph! Look who's here!'

The town was, of course, largely Catholic. So when I heard one of our teachers being less than polite about priests I was half scandalised, half amused. It was a bit of a shock when he wouldn't call them Father Paddy or Father Jack, but used the surname only—very disrespectful, which was unusual. And I remember my teacher Peadar McCann, from Newry, talking about a priest on the Meath side of the river, and referring to him as a 'real' priest, with a real vocation, not like some of the others who were in it for the standing and the comfortable living it gave.

'A priest in the family' was a source of great pride. The very occasional young man who decided it wasn't for him after a year or two in the seminary and came home again had to live down being called 'a spoiled priest' for years after. It was a cruel term of contempt, a great trial for the family and the recipient suffered as a 'marked man'.

Criticism of the clergy was muted and confined to liberal thinkers like the teachers and the occasional independent-minded business man. From them you might hear that the ambitious parish priest of St Peter's in the north of the town was grooming himself for a bishopric. But this sort of gossip was confined to a small circle. In general, the priests were regarded with a mixture of respect and caution. It didn't do to get the name of being a critic of the Church.

I sang in the church choir and my memory is that it included boys only. We attended practice under Eddy Lamb, choirmaster and organist, a very small, nervous man, regarded by us with amused tolerance. We welcomed the occasional High Mass which brought us sixpence each. A wedding High Mass could net us a half-crown from the groom or the father of the bride, if they were in generous mood. It was good money then.

We were conscious of a few Protestants (some even attended the Christian Brothers School); the banks, for instance, were mostly Protestant owned, as were other large businesses such as Murdochs, the builders providers. Protestants and Catholics mingled freely in the rowing and tennis clubs, but there was a strong sense that they were somehow 'different'.

We used to think that our neighbours, the Abernethys, were typical Protestants. The father, Alec, was the Head Postmaster. The family was by our standards small, just two boys, Victor and Mervyn. Although his salary was if anything less than my father's, Alec was a thrifty, saving man, and this enabled him to send his boys to boarding school in Dublin and later Victor was able to become a doctor through the College of Surgeons and Mervyn became a curate in the Church of Ireland. Of course, rearing large Catholic families like our nine cost more than the rearing of the small Protestant families. My sister May used to spend holidays with the the Abernethys in England when Alec retired there.

Other neighbours who lived not too far away had a renowned spring well in their back garden and I was often dispatched with a quart can to get a fill of the cold, pure water with a taste and flavour deserving of the adjectives bestowed on vintage champagne by wine buffs. Or so we thought, anyway. If you met someone coming back with a full can and you wished to have his or her company, you would say, 'Spill out and come back'. A ritual spilling of a cupful signified 'Yes'. And if on your way uptown on a message you met someone special heading for home, you could say, 'Spill out and come back' and be well understood.

Despite their grim conditions, the lowest on the social scale could always muster a phrase to raise a laugh. On summer days there was always a dozen or so of the permanently unemployed around the Tholsel at the corner of Shop Street and West Street, sunning themselves, yarning and laughing. As the sun moved, so the group unconsciously shifted around the corner to follow it. Some families were burdened with a male member who was either lazy, idle by temperament, or had aspirations to be a poet and behaved as if the great world was panting to see his work. The usual, and unusually charitable, comment on this situation was, 'Ah, well, sure, it's a poor family that can't afford one gentleman'.

There was a lot of drinking going on in the town. But we as lads didn't go in for drinking—we wouldn't have been allowed even if we'd wanted to, and anyway we didn't have the money. It was the same with sex. There was one fellow in school who always had a sexy story or two, and claimed to have 'been there', and to know the local tarts. We didn't think much of him—handball, hurling and rowing were much more on our minds.

Some of the men—and not only the working men—would drink too much and beat their wives. We'd hear about it, and someone would say 'oh, he's a no-good'. It was a small town where everyone knew everyone, and there was of course a lot of gossip, not all of it very charitable. There was a lot of jealousy of the 'Who does she think she is?' kind. Status was important. For instance, where you sat for Mass depended on how much money you gave into the plate at the door: if you went to the middle aisle you were expected to put more in than if you went to the side. In the middle you'd put in a sixpence or a shilling. And then there were the characters including Jack, a famous begrudger. If you met him on a lovely sunny day and called out 'Lovely day Jack!' he'd reply 'Ye have yer share of it!' One of the sights of the town was Paddy Nolan, the bell-ringer and general church factotum. He was very fat, weighing at least twenty stone though only five feet nine. To get around town he had a special strongly-built tricycle, for, as we all agreed, an ordinary bicycle would simple buckle under his weight.

At the age of eighty-four, Jack McDonnell, the Harbour Master, was still patrolling the quays on his old bicycle, directing Captains new to Drogheda to their berths. When I asked, 'How does Jack keep going so fresh and well and he over eighty?' 'Well,' I was told, 'all his life, Jack has had only two speeds, Dead Slow and Stop.'

Another great waterside character was Micky Dan McGuirk, the skipper of the Harbour Commissioners' dredger, the *Moy*. Micky had a perpetual shake, head nodding in time with his arms and shoulders. Local tradition had it that when working aloft he had fallen from the top-gallant yard of a sailing ship in Buenos Aires. He missed the deck, luckily, went down one side of the ship, came up the other and was hauled back on board. When he came to, he had the shakes. That was the story, but shakes or no, it was a treat to see Micky Dan going aboard, up a long, narrow gangplank like those used by the coal heavers, the plank bouncing up and down, his head and shoulders keeping time and Micky Dan keeping his balance as gracefully as a tight-rope walker. Men with no disability would think twice of 'walking the plank' to board and we young, active boys thought it no small feat either.

The favoured among us were taken by Micky Dan on his trips down the river and out to sea, steering north to a point off Clogher Head, where he would open the bilges and deposit the thick mud from the river. The spot was carefully chosen so that the tide would carry the spoil away from the coast. Sometimes Micky would let one of us steer the unwieldy vessel, showing us how to watch her bow and 'give her a spoke or two on the wheel now and then so that she kept a straight course.'

He lived in Baltray at the mouth of the Boyne on the north side and often walked home. A neighbour gave him a lift in his Ford one day. 'I'll steer for a while to give you a spell.' 'But you've never driven a motor car, Micky.' 'But what's the difference from steering a ship. You just give her a spoke or two to keep her straight.'

Drogheda was not a very political town, nor were we a particularly political family. As boys, of course we used to play Republicans against Free Staters—throwing stones at the other side, and occasionally building mini-forts to attack and defend. I was always on the Republican side.

Being a seaport, there was of course a brothel, though I didn't realise this until I had long left. I saw it referred to by John Ryan, when he described visiting Drogheda. It fronted as a huxter's shop, where you could get five apples for a ha'penny, that kind of thing, and it was known as Smiler Kelly's from the two attractive young women who lived in the house behind the shop and had a welcoming smile for all and sundry, including indeed schoolboys like ourselves walking past who smiled back in all innocence. If we were coming home late at night, from choir practice or the like, there'd be music and singing coming from the shop and whoever was with us, the adult, would laugh and say, 'Oh, there's a foreign ship in town, they are entertaining.'

I have no bad memories of school at the local Christian Brothers. Six strokes on the hand with the 'leather', a thick heavy strap, was a painful punishment but it was not too difficult to watch yourself and avoid it. There were quite a few boys who took pride in their ability to bear the punishment stoically so as not to give satisfaction to the Brother, others yelled their heads off and laughed when safely back in their seats.

The Brothers were not the only ones administering corporal punishment. It was common in all schools and in many homes, and was resorted to much more freely than in recent times. Against that background it is unfair to single out the Brothers as if they were the only offenders. Unruly boys, and there was always at least one in every class, could make life a misery for unfortunate lay teachers such as 'Kruger' Sheridan who suffered for years from one Eamon Delaney. The wags of the town delighted in thinking up nicknames for their neighbours. Eddy Sheridan was born during the Boer War and his father, like many Irishmen at the time, was a strong supporter of the Boers against the 'tyrannical British Empire'. He praised the Boer leader, Oom Paul Kruger, night and day and when his son was born the local wags immediately christened him 'Kruger'. The name stuck and was used to the extent that many barely remembered his real name. He taught Mathematics and Geography to my class, which included Eamon Delaney from near Bettystown, where his father owned a substantial farm. As well as ranching, he bred horses and had produced a winner of the Grand National. Eamon was a big, strong, hardy boy who cycled the four miles to school every day, come rain or sun. He had no interest in the Kruger's quadratic equations or the wonders of the Grand Canyon, but was just putting in the time until he could leave and join his father in schooling the horses. In class he exercised his wit at Kruger's expense.

'Sir, if you slipped at the edge of the Grand Canyon, how long would it take you to fall all the way?'

The class would titter. Eamon was in form.

'That's a stupid question, Delaney, and only a stupid fellow would go near the edge.'

'But I'd like to know, Sir. Would you have time to make an Act of Perfect Contrition before you hit the bottom?'

The class would explode in laughter at this.

Kruger Sheridan was a tall, thin, highly-strung man, an easy mark for the likes of Eamon Delaney. He was smoking fifteen cigarettes a day when Delaney started his harassment and as the months wore on, his smoking went up to twenty a day and then to twenty-five and he developed a shake in his hand when he attempted to write on the blackboard. When he was smoking thirty a day and the shake was worse it was clear that he was on the verge of a nervous breakdown. Time came to his rescue. Delaney reached the age for leaving school and the Kruger started to live again. The cigarettes were no longer so necessary, the shake gradually grew less and he even began to put on weight. In a few years he was back to his old self.

More years passed until one day he was enrolling new pupils.

'What's your name?'

'Peter O'Brien, sir.'

'Where are you from?'

'Tullyallen, sir'.

'And what's your name?'

'Thomas Gogarty, sir'.

'And where are you from?'

'Mell, sir.'

'You, what's your name?'

'Eamon Delaney, sir.'

'Where are you from?'

'Bettystown, sir.'

'Eamon Delaney from Bettystown! What's your father's name?'

'They call him Eamon Delaney, sir.'

'Eamon Delaney from Bettystown!'

The Kruger blessed himself, 'In the name of the Father, Son and Holy Ghost, have I to go through all that again!'

We were fortunate to have, in Peadar McCann, a lay teacher of rare quality, devoted to his pupils and possessing the true teacher's art of being able to impart his own delight in and love for the subjects he taught. From him I learned to appreciate Irish and English prose and poetry and he gave me an abiding source of enjoyment which has truly been an enrichment of life. However, the respect most of the boys had for him did not deter them from having some fun in his class.

There was a boy in fourth year called Swaine and one day when another boy, reading Milton's *Lycidas*, aloud, came to the line:

'How well could I have spared for thee, young swain', the entire class pointed at Swaine and said in unison, 'Young swain, young swain' and young Swaine blushed a bright red at this attention. When it came to the next reader's turn, he 'stumbled' over the line:

'The tufted crow-toe and the pale jessamine' which he rendered as: 'The crufted toe-toe and the pale jessie's mine' to the titters of his class mates.

But these were minor occasional mischiefs compared to the continual baiting of the poor Kruger and Peadar McCann disposed of them with a dismissive 'Don't flatter yourselves you can improve on Milton'.

On one occasion a brash sixteen-year-old, Eddie McQuillan, went too far. We had begun *The Merchant of Venice* and McQuillan, was reading the opening street conversation in which Gratiano, chiding the merchant Antonio for turning melancholy, exclaims:

> *'Why should a man, whose blood is warm within,*
> *Sit like his grandsire, cut in alabaster?'*

In a loud, strong voice, McQuillan declaimed

> *'Why should a man whose blood is warm within,*
> *Sit like his grandsire, a yalla bastard?'*

and he launched into the next line over uproar from the class. McCann quickly silenced him with a furious 'Out, out to the line' pointing to the wall. McQuillan spent the rest of the class standing against the wall until a Brother came and after a word with McCann, administered six 'stingers' to the offender with his leather strap and then sent him home.

A new games master, Brother O'Farrell, arrived from Kilkenny and coming from that home of hurling naturally thought it was the finest field game in the world and would do wonders for the boys. Despite the misgivings of some of the mothers who could see their darlings arriving home with split noses and battered heads, he succeeded in getting permission to introduce it. Teams were selected from fourth, fifth and sixth years and if at first we were slow and awkward, confidence soon developed and we wielded our camáns with increasing skill and vigour. A few years on, a school team competed with honour in the Leinster Schools and Colleges championships.

A new boy arrived, Dan Dunne, a fourteen-year-old from Kilkenny where he was born and reared, and his natural skill as a hurler filled us with jealousy and wonder. When the cricket outside our house began to pall, we thought of a challenge to test our new hurling skills by trying to hit the sliotar over the Viaduct. Dan Dunne was the only one of us who ever succeeded. There were boys who were bigger and stronger than him but they could not match the power and grace of his seeming effortless swing which sent the ball soaring up and over like a swallow on the wing. Dan went on to win an all-Ireland medal with Kilkenny to our pride and joy.

Those grassy acres, 'where we sported and played' are now covered by sheds and warehouses, and the front door of Riverside has been 'embellished' with a totally out of character door-case and architrave. *Sic transit . . .*

My great friend at that time was Paddy Murray, son of a local GP. Paddy had great energy and stamina and persuaded me to go on long walks with him on Sunday afternoons. He set a spanking pace and people stared at us as we pounded along as if we were competing in an Olympic race. We covered about sixteen miles in a little over three hours and I was quite stiff on the Monday following, but unrelenting Paddy would call for me the next Sunday and we would explore another part of rural Meath or Louth. His father was a widower and at fourteen Paddy was sent to board at St Patrick's College in Armagh but he was home for the summer holidays and swimming in the Boyne or on Laytown beach took the place of the walks. Then nothing would do him but that we should go for a swim on Christmas Day. We cycled five miles to Laytown, undressed, ran out across the beach and waded in. It was bitingly cold with an east wind clipping the waves but I had to follow Paddy out until we got to water deep enough for swimming. There was no shelter from the wind as we dressed and even cycling back home as fast as we could, I didn't get properly warm again until comfortably in front of a good fire in Riverside. Home for the Easter break, Paddy said we must honour St Patrick by going swimming on his feast day and so we did. But that finished me with cold weather swimming.

But he did involve me in another swimming exploit. Local swimmers regarded a swim from Clogher Head to Dunany Point, a distance of about six miles in the open sea, as a great challenge, their answer to the English Channel swim. When Paddy heard about it and that none of them had succeeded, he instantly decided that we should have a go, and set about organising it. So on a fine sunny Sunday in August three of us set off on our bicycles on the eight and a half miles from Drogheda, Paddy, myself and Jack O'Brien, a draper's assistant aged about twenty. We had sense enough to arrange with two Clogher Head fishermen to escort us in a row boat and were joined by Tommy Lawless, another local, a burly lad in his early twenties, regarded as a great swimmer by his Clogher Head neighbours.

The Pier on a Sunday was a favourite place for family groups and their friends to go walking and in the late afternoon dances were held there, with the music supplied by a 'squeeze box' and a fiddle or two. When we four swimmers appeared in our togs, ready to dive in, we got encouraging cheers from some and doubtful head shakings from others. Off we set but whatever about the others, I had no illusions or ambition about making it to Dunany Point. As we got out into deep water, it began to feel very cold and our burly friend had the advantage over us of a generous covering of flesh. The sea was choppy, not too bad, not really rough, but still it was difficult to avoid getting a mouthful from time to time. After nearly an hour and swimming about three miles, the cold began to get to me and I decided to give up. I was the first to be hauled into the boat and I was very glad to give myself a good rub with my towel, dress and take a turn at an oar to warm myself. That left Jack, Paddy and our well-endowed friend, Tommy. Paddy stuck it out for another mile and then joined me in the boat. We were both getting anxious about Jack and urged him to come on board. He shook his head but it was only too clear from the way his arms were flailing that he was getting exhausted so we rowed close to him and pulled him aboard. He lay on the floorboards and his limbs seemed to go rigid. We rubbed and dried him but he kept on shivering for quite a while.

Tommy kept going for another half-hour but the cold was getting to him too and he very reluctantly gave up when only a few hundred yards from Dunany Point. We made good time back to Clogher Pier, but Jack was still shivering and seemed to have little control over his arms and legs. Paddy and I held him up between us and walked him up and down the pier. He looked for all the world as if he'd had too much to drink and our unsteady progress drew scandalised looks and comments. When he had recovered somewhat, we succeeded in getting him up on his bicycle and with Paddy holding his handlebar on one side and I doing the same on the other, we wobbled our way back to Drogheda. Fortunately there was very little motor traffic those days and what there was did not go nearly as fast as today's, so we made it safely home and delivered Jack to his landlady. He took a long time to recover completely, I heard afterwards, paying dearly for his attempt to be as good as Tommy Lawless.

Home from his last day at boarding school, Paddy startled me by saying he was going to be a priest. Until then, he had given no sign of having a vocation. So off he went to join the Holy Ghost Fathers and I lost sight of him for some years. He wanted to be a missionary, but it turned out that he was a gifted teacher, especially of English, and his superiors decreed that he would serve them better in that capacity. So he remained in Ireland, teaching in Rockwell College and then St Mary's College, Rathmines. Many years later, when our youngest, Peter, had reached twelve, Paddy had become President of St Mary's and I was very glad to put Peter in his care. He was happy there, turned out to be very good at rugby and played on the school team that won the Leinster Senior Schools Cup, scoring a try and kicking a penalty in the final. I have never seen anybody, old or young, before or since, who looked so blissfully happy as he did going up for his medal.

Paddy died in his early seventies, after being knocked down by a motor-car when crossing the road. His injuries were quite severe and he never really recovered from them.

While we were growing up, in the 1920s, Drogheda Rowing Club had some splendid crews. On fine summer evenings, the townspeople came out in their hundreds to stroll along the banks and watch the crews training. By today's standards they were not big men but they were wiry and had great stamina. Some were sons of farmers, others worked in the town. In 1928 they beat a fancied Trinity Eight at Islandbridge. It was said to be the finest Senior Eight Trinity had put on the water for many years and the following week they were going to Henley Royal Regatta with high hopes. Drogheda had a style of rowing all their own, long powerful strokes and an almost leisurely sweep of the blades back for the next stroke, with the blades seeming to butter the water. Watching them, my father said, 'They go out the full length of the oar.' Trinity led off in fine style and took an early lead. This did not seem to bother the Drogheda crew. Their long, unhurried strokes kept the Trinity boat within a length and from the half-way mark they began to wear their opponents down. Foot by foot they crept up and Trinity's faster stroke was unavailing. The Drogheda crew rowed past them without quickening their rate of striking, only seeming to put more power behind each stroke, and crossed the finishing line half a length ahead. It was a famous victory and the Trinity crew was devastated. Beaten before they even left for Henley!

The Drogheda crew went on to win the Senior Eights Championship of Ireland at the Boyne in 1930. They beat a Trinity crew in a heat and a City of the Tribes crew from Galway by a quarter of a length in the final. A commentator said, 'Boyne rowing never had a finer hour.' A few years later, in Dublin, I took up competitive rowing myself, with some success. The Drogheda Club disbanded years ago and the fine clubhouse lies derelict.

On summer evenings I played handball with some of the weavers against the wall of Usshers' Linen Mills not far from our house. We played a lot of handball. There were courts at school and locally—it was a popular game. Some of the players were splendid. If you were a skilled player you could beat your opponent by aiming the ball to hit the bottom of the front wall, in the angle with the ground so that it came back on the ground, at full speed. It was unplayable in that position. This was called 'butting the ball' and won a point every time. Only the most expert could manage it. We played with a soft ball. The hard ball was for older experienced players, the palms of whose hands had been hardened by years of the soft ball. The balls were the same size, a little bigger than a golf ball. You had to be able to use both hands, otherwise a crafty opponent would soon spot your weak one, and play the ball to it, to your disadvantage. If your return struck either side wall or the ground before it hit the front wall, that was a foul. You called out 'Look sharp' when serving the

19th ball and 'Game ball' for the 20th which won the game.

Afterwards we would retire to one of the weaver's cottages to play cards. Here I learned how to play Spoil Five and Twenty-Five in a very demanding school. Five or six of us sat round a small table and after each trick, the cards were left in an untidy heap on the table until that game was played out. You had to watch carefully where each card came from as the players were a yard or so away from the dim light of an oil lamp. When a card came flying in from the dimness you had to register instantly, 'That was Micky, holding ten. Leave him be.' Tommy was the one to watch, 'don't let him rise to twenty'. If you let a man 'rising twenty' take a trick when you had the beating of him, their disgust was freely vented. And you heard more if he took the next trick and the game.

'Did you not know he had the fingers?' (the five of trumps, the best card in the pack).

'Do they not tell you at that school of yours that you should play for the board?'

The weavers' memory was phenomenal. They took a keen delight in the tactics of the game and sighed with pleasure when they had two or three 'twenty men' fighting for the last trick and the game. Years later when I played in Dublin, few opponents could match my skill at Spoil Five or Twenty-Five, acquired through those years of tough tutoring.

We often went swimming at Mornington, only three miles away, an easy ride on our bicycles. We swam in a pool not far from Baldy Reynold's cottage. It was called 'The Minister's Hole', having been the favourite resort of a man of the cloth, long since dead. Approached by a short causeway from the main road, it was just inside the river wall and was filled and emptied by the tide. So we had a pool of sea water, fresh and clean every day. Captain Lyons, a local retired sea-captain, joined us most days and entertained us with stories of his adventures afloat. He was shipwrecked once and had spent days and nights waiting and hoping for rescue. Keeping warm in the ship's lifeboat was the big problem and he told us gravely 'Most of your body heat escapes through your head and I spent hours patting the top of my head', here followed a demonstration 'and then pulled my cap on tight and got some sleep'. My father dismissed him and his stories, 'that old cod', but Captain Lyons told his stories so well and so graphically that we, hero-worshipping schoolboys, believed every word.

When we were young, the family took off in the summer for Baltray, a very small village three miles away on the coast near to the mouth of the Boyne. We stayed in a thatched cottage belonging to a 'friend', as distant relatives were then called. We made the journey on a hay float, loaded with extra beds, tables and chairs needed for our numbers. On arrival, the first thing was to throw off our shoes and until we returned to Drogheda nearly three months later, we went barefoot. We went swimming in the sea two or three times a day and I thought that this relieved us from further obligation to wash but my mother soon put me right on that.

In later years we stayed in Skerries, the height of sophistication after Baltray. I think this was arranged by the older ones then working. I remember a 'fit up' group of singers and comedians who performed nightly and went round with the hat at intervals. Some of the songs brought guffaws from the young men standing in front of the makeshift stage while their girl friends tried to look disapproving. The saucy allusions were way above my head but I still remember a verse that went like this:

> *And as he met her at the station*
> *He was heard to say,*
> *Oh, we must have one more rum-tum-tum*
> *Before you go away.*

Another song was for the younger ones in the afternoons:

Barefoot days, when you were just a kid,
Barefoot days, O boys the things we did.
Slide and slide, till your pants got torn,
Then you had to go home and stay in your bed,
While your mother got busy with her needle and thread,
Oh, boy, what joy, we had in barefoot days.'

4 Up to Dublin

I left school in June 1930 without a clear idea of what I was going to do in life. My two older brothers had gone to sea, following the family tradition, and I was very attracted to the idea. Unfortunately world events, way outside my ken, ruled that out. The depression that followed the great Wall Street Crash of 1929 was having world-wide repercussions. International trade was worst hit, with the result that hundreds, if not thousands, of ships were laid up. There were no cargoes for them to carry and legions of Master Mariners, junior officers and sailors found themselves 'beached'. Luckily my brothers were well established by then and weathered the storm, but the prospects for a newcomer were simply nil.

So I had to look elsewhere. University was not an option without a scholarship and the only one available was the Easter Scholarship which was tenable only at teacher-training colleges. I had no desire to be a National Teacher under the jurisdiction of a parish priest. Drogheda had very little in the way of large companies, and what jobs there were generally went to relatives of existing employees. There were possibilities in the banks and insurance companies, but these jobs seemed to me very dull, and could entail many years waiting in a remote country sub-branch for promotion. In the end I joined the biggest employer of all, the Civil Service. Because of the Service's reasonable pay, security and prestige, these jobs were fiercely sought after, so there was a stiff competitive exam. Hundreds sat the examination and in those days only twenty or at most thirty appointments were made. However, I was successful and I ended up as an Executive Officer in the Land Commission.

I moved to Dublin to take up my new post in November, 1930. My parents came to Dublin a few months later, and I lived with them in Rathgar, first in a red-brick semi in Victoria Road, then in a mews house off Orwell Road, until I got married. Unfortunately, the 'glory days' of the Land Commission, when it had presided over massive shifts of land ownership from the old landlords to tenants, were over. The work was quite dull. Not that there weren't some characters to brighten the day. For instance, the Treaty of 1921 provided that civil servants could opt to retire on favourable terms or work out their remaining service with the new Irish administration. The Land Commission had a number of these ex-British civil servants. They had absorbed the outlook, ways and manners of their former mandarin superiors and some of them were very conscious that they were no longer officials in a great Empire but were serving a new administration in a small, poor and to them, backward country. They addressed each other in friendly terms as 'old man' and laced their minutes with Latin and French tags. *A fortiori*, and *ad hoc* and *faute de mieux* were favourites. Their integrity was above question and the confidentiality of official information was sacrosanct. They might say of some sharp practice 'Not cricket, old man', and a few, a very few exuded an air of superiority to the 'rough, rug-headed kerns' floundering in this new world, but there was plenty of value to be learned from them as well.

When in 1932 de Valera's Government abolished the Oath of Allegiance to the King, Republicans felt free to join the Civil Service and the Land Commission got its share. Many had lost their Government jobs on joining the fight for freedom. There were men who had fought in Flying Columns. One was said to have been the last to lay down his gun in West Cork. Many of the new entrants used the Irish form of their names and this always caused problems with the 'old British'. One committed Irish speaker refused the usual request for 'your name in English'.

'My name is MacGiollarnath, Mr Chadwick.'

'Yes, yes. I want it in English.'

'There is no English for it.'

'Nonsense, there has to be.'

'There's no English for Mussolini, Mr Chadwick, or for Balzac or Napoleon Bonaparte.'

'Well, your Christian name. You have one, I presume?'

'Yes, Mr Chadwick, it's Amhlaoibh.'

'Oh, go away! Give your particulars to Mr Murphy.'

It was certainly a strange mélange. It must be said for the 'old British' that they upheld the best traditions of their class.

There was a lady superintendent who kept a watchful eye on the women staff. Since women had to leave the service when they married, the majority of them were young women, girls, in fact. A girl from Mayo said to me one day 'Miss K. has forbidden us to wear sleeveless dresses in the summer. She says we would be rising the passions of the men.'

Some of the men relieved the tedium of their day from time to time by having fun with the stuffier of their colleagues. The room they worked in accommodated about thirty staff and this gave our 'playboys' an opportunity to engage in their favourite diversion. They would go to a phone at the far end of the room from their intended victim and one of them would phone him and pretend to be a TD.

'This is Deputy McGrath,' naming an obscure backbencher.

'Yes, Deputy.'

'I have a serious complaint to make against your department.'

'I'm sorry to hear that, Deputy.'

'You'll be sorrier still when I'm finished with you.'

And from there on the unfortunate man was treated to a barrage of abuse and complaints. They were in convulsions at his discomfiture and they could almost see the sweat breaking out on his face as he tried to mollify the irate Deputy, who ended the one-sided dialogue by threatening to report him to higher authority and banging down the phone. My 'playboys' would go back to their desks, refreshed, tedium banished and sit down to work again with renewed zeal. They were, it seemed to me, perfect exemplars of an observation by John B. Yeats in a letter to his son, the poet, W. B. 'A perfectly disinterested, an absolutely unselfish love of making mischief, mischief for its own dear sake, is an Irish characteristic.'

Dublin was exciting, certainly. There was the Abbey Theatre where I saw the great names at their best, F. J. McCormick, Barry Fitzgerald, Sarah Allgood, Ria Mooney and many others, in the plays of Shaw, O'Casey, Yeats et al. But the office work was dull and repetitive, and the days assumed a sameness that was mind-numbing.

For pastime, I joined the Dublin Rowing Club. Here I found a more rewarding variety of company. Rowing was as natural to me as walking after my days on the Boyne, and from the start I was always chosen as stroke oar. The stroke set the rate of striking and led the crew. In rowing, strength and weight are obviously important, a good big man will always beat a good small man, but skill is more so. A racing boat is about sixty feet long, with a canvas-covered bow six feet long, and has a two feet beam. It has a rounded hull and is only kept from capsizing by the four oars extended on each side. But the key to success in racing is timing: the eight oars MUST strike the water in unison to the micro-second so that the maximum weight and strength is applied to the blades. A blade late or early contributes little to the speed of the boat and may indeed impair it. At the end of the stroke, when the blade comes out of the water and the oarsman starts to move forward again on his sliding seat, the boat must be kept perfectly balanced to maintain maximum speed and it stays upright just as a bicycle does when in motion. The oarsman must learn to balance the boat, not to jerk or shift his weight in any way. 'Don't rock the boat' has a special meaning for oarsmen.

During this time Belvedere College asked the club to provide instruction in rowing for its senior pupils; the best of them were selected for the club's racing crews. In that way we ended up with very light crews—our schoolboys were all below ten stone—but they were very fast. At nearly twelve stone I was easily the biggest and strongest in our boat. These youngsters really did 'pull their weight'. Our crew were always much lighter than those we beat, to their astonishment and chagrin, but skill, timing and balance won out each time. It was a treat to meet opposing crews on dry land for the first time after we had beaten them, and see their jaws drop as we went up to collect our medals at the prize-giving. Those brawny broad-shouldered young men shook their heads in disbelief.

There were two schoolboys in our crew when we won a Gold Medal in the Tailteann Games in 1932. The Tailteann Regatta was held on the Boyne and it gave me particular pleasure to stroke a winning crew on my home waters. And no doubt, my knowledge of the river gave me extra confidence. Our racing tactics were well thought out. Most crews went for an early lead, arguing that once in front, their opponents would find it very difficult to take the lead from them. Our logic was that the crew in front, watching the one following them, set the pace and it was a waste of energy to try to pass them early on. Just don't let them get more than three-quarters of a length ahead, and lull them into thinking that we were trying our best and just hadn't the pace. If they began to draw further ahead, we would raise our rate well over 30-to-the minute in a sustained spurt, easing back when we got on terms again. Then when within a quarter of a mile from the finish, we would put in our effort, suddenly spurting to a high rate, taking them by surprise and usually drawing level before they could respond. We had not tired ourselves in fruitless attempts earlier to catch up and our sudden increase in pace was usually so unexpected as to, literally, put them off their stroke. This tactic saw us gain a lead of a few feet, but that was enough, we kept up the pace and they had no answer. And when Sinéad Jennings won a gold medal in the single sculls at the World Championshsips in Lucerne in August 2001, I was charmed when she described her racing tactics very much like our own of over sixty years before.

In July 1933 the *Irish Field* reported on our success in the Galway Regatta Junior Eights. There were four schoolboys in the crew.

> The races for the Menlo Challenge Cup were to my mind a personal triumph for H. J. Boylan of Dublin Rowing Club. In his first race against Shannon and Dublin University he had a lead at one period of two lengths but Trinity crept up and up while Boylan kept steadily on though he knew that his crew was faltering behind him. At 100 yards from the winning post he was a few feet down but Trinity cracked then and Boylan with a terrific ten just got home to seize the lead and win by a canvas. In the final, Dublin had a close race with Limerick Boat Club and just beat them by half a canvas, Boylan stroking them exceedingly well.

The elders in the club, men in their thirties and early forties, 'greybeards' to us nineteen- and twenty-year-olds, always spoke solemnly of rowing as a very tough, demanding sport. They described the agony of the last stages of a race as akin to the pangs of childbirth. According to them, few of the crews in the Oxford and Cambridge Boat Race survived beyond their thirties, such was the fearful strain imposed on their hearts. I was somewhat more than sceptical of this 'folklore'. In many hard-fought races I had never experienced the agony they described. And I remembered that the Earl of Iveagh, winner of the Diamond Sculls at Henley Regatta, was still going strong in his nineties. It would be described by psychologists and analysts today as an exercise in boosting the egos of both themselves and ourselves, they as heroic survivors of the challenge and we as their successors as upholders of the noble and élite sport for real men. It was complete codology.

Late in 1936, after some uninteresting years in the Land Commission, I went before a selection board open to the whole Civil Service and was appointed Staff Administration Officer in the ten-year-old Radio Éireann. The Broadcasting Service was then part of the Department of Posts and Telegraphs and was housed on the top floor of the GPO in O'Connell Street. We entered by Henry Street and went to the top of the building where there was a long corridor with offices off it: the three or four studios and the rehearsal room were above that again. The corridor walls were tiled for their full length up to a height of five feet on each side, with the sort of tiles very common in public conveniences. It was popularly called 'the longest lavatory in Dublin'.

On my first day in my new post I met Dr T. J. Kiernan, the Director and Frank Gallagher, his Deputy, who had been the first editor of the *Irish Press*, and was later to become Director of the Government Information Bureau. Both were friendly and welcoming, but I felt they were giving me a quick, sharp examination. Kiernan was a career diplomat who had been asked in 1935 to accept temporary secondment from the Department of External Affairs to straighten out Radio Éireann, then under severe criticism. Frank Gallagher, by profession a journalist, was a veteran of the struggle for independence. He was the first to tell me that I should never speak or write 'that so-and-so had taken the Republican side after the Treaty of 1921'. 'Remember,' he said, 'We *stayed* on the Republican side.' He was a devoted follower of de Valera.

Frank gave me a quick run-down on the staff of Radio Éireann. There were about fifty people in all: first the engineers, always sensitive to any criticism of the quality of the transmission, especially from 'head-in-air' writers and administrators; three or four programme staff such as Roibeárd Ó Faracháin, the Talks Officer, who kept the flag flying for fellow poets at programme conferences. Roibeárd became a Director of the Abbey within a couple of years of my joining Radio Éireann. John MacDonagh was in charge of drama; he was brother of Thomas, a signatory of the Proclamation of the Republic in Easter Week 1916, executed on 3 May, and had himself been 'out' in 1919–22. Then there were the announcers, the office staff and the orchestra, which was about 25-strong under the conductor, Captain J. M. Doyle from the Army School of Music, with Dr Vincent O'Brien as Director and Arthur Duff as his deputy, and Rhoda Coghill, accompanist and also highly regarded as a poet. A particularly important person was the Record Librarian, Miss Evans who lived in a room full of records and added to this collection continuously from new issues.

'You', said Frank 'will be the General Manager of Radio Éireann.' This seemed a tall order for one so young and comparatively inexperienced as I was but I soon found that it meant in practice that I was to be the right-hand man of the Director and Deputy Director and as third in the 'hierarchy' see to it that the organisation ran as smoothly as possible and achieved the best results, leaving them free to concentrate on programme planning and policy. At lunchtime (from 1.30 to 2.30) we broadcast weather, children's hour and some music; and then restarted at 6 pm and went on until 11 pm. There were plays, talks and music and news at 6.45 pm and 10.30 pm. While I was there Kiernan developed the policy of sponsored programmes to get over our chronic shortage of funds. A popular music programme was sponsored by the Sweep, and other big firms such as Jacobs were persuaded to sponsor a programme. The actors presenting these programmes were well paid, and became household names. The ordinary announcers read the news as well as doing continuity; they were often young briefless barristers, and did not give their names at this time.

On our own initiative we had regular plays, perhaps two or three a month. It was some years before the Radio Éireann Players were set up, so each play was cast from freelancers. Talks were given by the likes of Frank O'Connor, Micheál MacLiammóir, Seán Ó Faoláin and Padraig Colum. Meeting these people was one of the bonuses of working in the station. News was nothing like as slick a performance as today: broadcast twice a day, the bulletins were put together by a News Editor, an assistant and a News Correspondent in Cork, with the occasional reports from stringers around the country. Most of the news was lifted from the newspapers and the BBC—funds hardly stretched to the ordinary news services such as Reuters.

There was more than one strong personality on the staff (the equivalent of today's 'Big Egos'), but I enjoyed the general atmosphere of freedom and 'make-it-up-as-we-go along' that I would never have met in the usual Government department. At the weekly programme conference every Monday morning there were brisk, lively exchanges punctuated by gales of laughter when a reputation was shattered in a phrase. Having been thrown in at the deep end, I soon learned when to be wary and when a forthright opinion was called for. Dr Kiernan kept a sharp eye out for 'clique building', a programme head keeping the same people far too long on programmes. At one conference he asked how a certain series was being received? Miss A. replied brightly,

'It's going very well.'

'How do you know?'

'We're getting plenty of letters.'

'Could we see some of them, could you bring them down from your office?'

'Oh, yes,' with a startled look.

Miss A. departed. Ten minutes passed, then fifteen.

'It's taking a long time to write a few letters,' said Kiernan dryly.

Miss A. returned, clutching a few sheets of note paper. The series was dropped.

Dr Vincent O'Brien, Director of Music, was a charming, friendly, unsuspicious man.

'What have you for us this week, Doctor?'

'We have booked a series of recitals by some new, small groups.'

'That sounds interesting.'

'Yes, on Monday we have the Gresham Quartet, on Wednesday the Shelbourne Trio, on Friday the Grafton Ensemble.'

'Vincent', said Frank Gallagher, laughing, 'do you not know that these are all the same players ringing the changes?'

Kiernan had put in four gruelling years 'sorting out Radio Éireann' and was anxious to resume his career in the Diplomatic Service. One day early in August 1939 when I had been over two years there, he said to me 'You've heard the rumours, I suppose, that I have got a posting abroad? Well, it's true, I've been appointed Minister Plenipotentiary to Germany.' He was clearly delighted and I congratulated him. 'I'll be leaving in a few weeks,' he said. 'There will be an announcement then.' He went on, 'This will mean changes here, of course. Frank will move up as Director in my place. You have done very well since you came here. You have a very unusual combination of imagination and executive ability and you are the obvious choice to succeed Frank as Deputy Director.' His words opened a welcome and gratifying prospect. I was only twenty-seven, very much younger than Frank, whom I liked and admired. I was sure we would work well together. I would learn from his wide experience and with luck could end up as Director before I was forty.

But Europe was in turmoil: Hitler invaded Poland on 1 September 1939 and on 3 September 1939, Neville Chamberlain announced to the world that the British Empire was at war with Germany. Some days later Kiernan came into my room, sat down, smiled ruefully, and said, 'I'm not going to Germany.' He saw that I was taken aback at this extraordinary news. 'It's the war,' he said. 'How's that? We're neutral.' I said. 'True, ' he said, 'but the accrediting letter I present when taking up my post must be signed by the King of England. Can you see King George VI addressing "his trusty and well-beloved friend, Adolf Hitler", and commending me to his care?' So that was that, *bhí deire leis an aisling dhíl*, the hopes of each of us were dashed. This was the second time world-historical affairs had thrown me off course.

Kiernan had to wait for his posting until late in 1941 when he was appointed to the Holy See. The position about accrediting letters was changed with the declaration of the Republic in 1949, and since then the monarch of England has no longer any function in the matter.

The 'phoney war' at first did not have any impact on our day-to-day activities in Radio Éireann, but we soon noticed that there was a tightening of the purse strings. At this time all programmes were broadcast live. It was not until a special propaganda service broadcasting to the US was set up that programmes were recorded on large wax disks. They were not broadcast until 3–4 am to allow for the time difference with the USA East Coast but were recorded during usual station working hours. I arranged that the broadcasters be paid at once as I saw no point in delaying—after all they had done their job—and this made me very popular with them! The subtle relations between Britain and neutral Ireland during the war nearly got us into serious trouble. Frank O'Connor, then living in Dublin, had been asked to broadcast a talk for the BBC, and as a matter of routine courtesy we had allowed the programme to be broadcast from our studios. Someone, and I never knew whether it was the German Representative in Ireland or a hard-line Fianna Fáiler, complained about this to Dev, who passed the concern on to Dr Kiernan. I well remember how worried this experienced diplomat was in those touchy times—but the storm blew over, as these things do. Another symptom of troubled times was the fact that a soldier was put on guard in the ante-room to the studios to prevent the IRA from seizing the microphones and broadcasting to the nation. On one tremendous occasion, whether out of boredom or drink, the soldier let fly with a bullet down the length of the office corridor, to the terror of the workers. After that we had a nice peaceful Garda Sergeant to protect us.

Several of the staff who were good linguists were transferred to Censorship and were not replaced. The Government began recruitment to the Army, ambitious plans for new programmes somehow lost momentum and gradually the whole organisation seemed to be winding down, although this was probably due more to the general uncertainty about what the future held then anything else. News took on an increased importance and records began to figure more and more. It was a big change from the liveliness of previous years. To relieve this tedium I wrote a radio play about a crafty river pilot on the Boyne and his machinations to corner most of the pilotage and the good fees that went with them. It was based on a real life pilot and his running battle with the Harbour Board, which included my father. Being very conscious of Dr Kiernan's attitude to any suggestion of favouritism, I submitted it under a pen-name Henry Coleman, to the head of Drama, John McDonagh. He accepted it by return of post. I walked down the corridor to his room and announced to him 'Henry Coleman, at your service.' John was taken aback but said, 'It's a very good play' and it was duly broadcast. With the ice broken, I wrote further scripts, including one on sea shanties and a dramatisation of *The Moonstone*, a thriller by Wilkie Collins, nineteenth-century master of suspense.

One day in 1940 I was listening on the monitor in my room to a rehearsal of a verse-speaking programme directed by Austin Clarke. I heard a woman's voice reading 'The Three-Cornered Field' by F. R. Higgins. It is a poem of lost love, of betrayal. It was read with great feeling, the reader *was* the girl lamenting her loss.

The Three-Cornered Field

By a field of the crab-trees my love and I were walking
And talking most sweetly to each other;
In the three-cornered field, we walked in early autumn,
And these were the words of my lover:

'A poor scholar like me who never took to girling
Finds book-knowledge such a bitter morsel—
Yet were I a clergyman, wise in holy learning,
O I'd make your wild beauty my gospel.'

And softly, softly his words were moving through me—
Coaxing as a fife, crying like a fiddle—
That I heard my heart beat, as dew beat on the stubble;
And the twilight was then lying with us.

In that three-cornered field, while the moon was whitely filling
The grass there gave hunger to our passion,
And so said my love: 'With the new year, let me give you
The red marriage ring for a hansel.'

Since then I never hear him, but soon O I'll see him
Just darken God's doorway on a Sunday—
Yes, darken God's doorway as he darkened my reason
And narrowed my daylight last summer.

So again by the crab-trees, the grass is lean with autumn
Where again I'll be waiting for my lover;
And while he'll never know it, with him I'll go walking,
Although he is wed to another.

I said, 'I must meet the owner of that voice'. This was easily contrived, and that was how I came to meet and marry Patricia

Clancy. Her family came from the North, though they then lived in Dublin. She was a graduate of the Abbey School of Acting, then directed by Lennox Robinson, and was a well-known broadcaster, actress and journalist and would later become the author of a well-received history of the United Arts Club. We became engaged within a few months.

As Radio Éireann wound down I was offered a promotion, and returned to the mainstream Civil Service, first for a brief spell in the newly-founded Department of Supplies under Seán Lemass, and then in 1942 back to the Department of Lands. I was sorry to leave Radio Éireann, but as I was getting married the salary increase was very welcome and I told myself that the war could not last for ever and that surely I could find my way back to Radio Éireann. It was not to be and my foray into writing was perforce abandoned when I left the station, not to be resumed until leisure and opportunity came with retirement from 'the day job'.

Patricia and I were married on 18 September 1941. For our honeymoon we went to Port na Blagh in Donegal, travelling all the way to Dunfanaghy by rail and ending up on a train of very small carriages on a branch line long since closed. Donegal then seemed very remote, cut off from the rest of the Free State and difficult of access. In Port na Blagh—the Port of the Famous—we stayed in Walsh's comfortable family hotel and enjoyed the sunshine of an Indian summer. There we met Ulrica Donnell from Strabane, who was to become a lifelong friend (and babysitter). She was then taking a holiday after the death of her father; quite soon she moved to Dublin and became 'Lady Almoner' in Baggot Street Hospital. (This wonderful title has now been replaced by the mundane 'Social Worker'.) We started our lives together in a flat on Merrion Road in Ballsbridge opposite the RDS and before long we moved to an old house in Dundrum, which was then rurally detached from Dublin. Annaville House had a walled garden of half an acre, called 'the orchard' because it had apple, plum and pear trees, a wall of loganberries and a greenhouse where we grew a hundred tomato plants. The large old house, beside the Central Mental Hospital, had been converted into two semi-detached houses and was surrounded by several acres of rough grass and woodland, with a drive from the public road. The other half was occupied by John Jordan, a Principal Officer in the Department of Finance, his wife May, a teacher, and their children Mary and Tommy. In the acres around the house our own brood, the young Jordans and other neighbours' children found an exciting playground. We kept a dozen hens and a couple of ducks so that as well as fruit and vegetables we had plenty of fresh eggs. War shortages were beginning to bite, but with plenty of hard work we lived well. Even the problem of bad turf was surmounted as I carried out some judicious tree pruning. By the time we left Dundrum, in 1952, our four children Hugo, Anna, Kato and Peter had been born. Patricia, with astonishing energy, combined caring for them with continuing her multi-talented career.

In the winter months I often went into Dublin on the old Harcourt Street line. The steam train took twelve minutes to get to Harcourt Street Station, stopping at Milltown and Ranelagh stations. On the train would be four acquaintances, young men of my own age. One morning a pack of cards was produced and the owner said, 'What about a few quick games of Poker?' We all jumped at this, bets were fixed at a figure to match our very modest earnings and off we went. The more sedate and older passengers in the carriage, each with his *Irish Times* at full spread, at first regarded this caper of ours with unfeigned disfavour, but we were so immersed in the calling and bluffing that they soon retreated again to their sacred morning read. We were not noisy, one does not talk much at Poker, and I think they came to envy us our obvious carefree enjoyment.

The closure of the Harcourt Street line in 1959 brought a huge outcry, but CIE could not be made to relent, and to ensure that the decision could not be easily reversed, they knocked down the railway bridge across the main Dundrum road, though the service is now being replaced by the Luas.

Two incidents made the first year of marriage one of ups and downs. Of course the 'Emergency' was on, though by then the fear of being invaded (by the Germans, or perhaps the British or even the Americans) had begun to fade. I did my stint as an Air Raid Warden for Radio Éireann, though in the absence of actual air raids this was more a theoretical responsibility than an actual one.

Soon after the wedding my father entered Dr Steevens' hospital for treatment for an enlarged prostate. The surgeon was Arthur Chance of a well known medical family. A few days after he had returned home following what seemed successful treatment I went to see him. I still had my latchkey and I let myself in and looked into the drawing room. He was sitting on the sofa, my mother beside him with her arms round him and I saw with some alarm the tears streaming down his weather-beaten face. He had just been told that he must go back to the hospital for further treatment. He was nearly eighty, he was frightened and my mother was comforting him. Fortunately, the second visit proved successful and he lived for five years more until he had a heart attack. I was with him some hours before he died and as he lay seemingly almost in a coma I heard him say in a whisper 'God be thanked for all his mercies'. My eldest sister, May, told me my mother cried herself to sleep for months after. Their marriage was clearly a good one and all seven of us who married have been equally fortunate and happy. At our wedding Patricia smiled as she saw my father determinedly make his way to stand beside my mother for the photographs. And later he made sure to sit beside her at the reception.

The second excitement of our first year was that quite soon after our marriage I was struck down with diphtheria, which was very dangerous in those days before antibiotics. I was so sick that the ambulance men had to lift me down the stairs from our flat on a stretcher. I then spent a couple of months in a ward full of children (the normal sufferers from the disease) in Baggot Street Hospital, with Patricia visiting bringing me such goodies as she could find. If it was very boring for me—and it was—it was worse for Patricia, left alone in the flat. The last straw came one night when a mouse ran across her pillow! The next day Dr Synge (cousin to the playwright) had a visit from a very determined patient's wife. By luck, just then the lab in Trinity declared my blood free of infection and I was released.

5 The 'sweet and kingly'

After Patricia and I became engaged I met Rupert Strong, a friend of hers, then an undergraduate at Trinity College. He later practised as a psychoanalyst; his wife Eithne was a noted poet. At that time Rupert was also working with Cahills, who were then publishers as well as printers. He shared rooms in Trinity with the eccentric R. B. McDowell, and Patricia had lunch there from time to time. Rupert was reading Modern Literature and told me that this involved attendance at only four or five hour-long lectures weekly in the seven weeks of lectures in each of the three terms, Michaelmas, Hilary and Trinity. The undergraduates were treated as adults not as glorified schoolchildren expected to attend every lecture and take down reams of notes. Results depended on their own intelligence and efforts and not on memorising and regurgitating voluminous notes taken at many lectures. (This approach perhaps explains why undergraduates at Trinity as at Oxford say that they are 'reading' philosophy or geography or science or whatever, not that they are 'studying' or 'doing' the subject.)

My interest was aroused. I realised that it would be possible for me to continue in my full-time job and take a degree, mostly by studying at night. Rupert introduced me to his tutor, Francis La Touche Godfrey and in 1941 soon after we married I was duly enrolled. Trinity had only 1,300 students then and classes were unbelievably small as compared to conditions today. I registered for a Moderatorship (honours degree) in Modern Literature. Two languages were required for major study and I chose Irish and English.

There were only twenty-two in the English class and eight in the Irish so we had very close attention from our lecturers. Listening and learning was a pleasure in those conditions, and I cannot forget that it was Patricia who opened the doors of Trinity to me.

The famous 'ban' on attendance of Catholics at TCD without their bishops' express permission dated from a Maynooth Statute of 1875. It was reiterated by Archbishop McQuaid in his Lenten Pastoral of 1944, when Trinity Term lectures ending my third year at TCD had just begun. I had a further year to go and after some cogitation decided to apply for the Archbishop's consent for my continued attendance, although in the event of a refusal I had no real intention of abandoning it after three year's work. The Archbishop's permission did not come until 27 March 1945, when I had only one more term to attend. It was a form letter, with blank spaces for my name and address and the courses in TCD. The ban was enforced until 1970, when Rome, at the request of the Irish Hierarchy, sanctioned the repeal of the Maynooth statute. Dr McQuaid probably felt a special responsibility in respect of this statute since TCD was in his diocese. There was no great rush of students from the hills of Donegal or the bogs of Mayo so other bishops apparently did not feel any necessity to speak.

Kerry is a special case. A Sizarship or Scholarship to TCD was founded in 1888 open only to natives of Kerry. The present Professor of Modern Literature in TCD, Dr Brendan Kennelly, was a Reid scholar.

Although participation in College activities outside lectures was necessarily limited to evenings, I joined 'the Hist', the Cumann Gaelach and the Sailing Club and contributed to the College magazine, *TCD Miscellany.* I soon found that Rupert and myself were not the only undergrads who were working their way through College. A few years before, another civil servant with whom I was to have contacts later, the late Tim O'Driscoll, had rooms in college and captained the rugby team before graduating BA. He later became our ambassador in the Netherlands before resigning to become the first Director-General of Bord Fáilte. Older students were accepted without comment as a normal feature of the College scene and we received every facility and consideration from our tutors. 'Tutor' is rather a misleading title. The tutor does not teach, he or she is intended to stand *in loco parentis*, offering general direction and encouragement. The ideal tutor becomes your guide, philosopher and friend as well as your intermediary with the Board. In Godfrey we had a tutor whose exceptional care for our interest was almost fatherly. He cycled into College every day from his house in Raglan Road and maintained his equilibrium while leaning very low down the left-hand side of his machine, an eccentric feat which drew amused and admiring attention.

After four years study I duly graduated with a First Class Moderatorship. The conferring, Commencements, in the Examination Hall, turned out to be a rather rowdy affair. The Chancellor and Fellows were ranged on a platform and the candidates, numbering about a hundred and thirty, sat facing them. The back of the hall was occupied by a noisy crowd of undergraduates and friends. When the Provost rose to begin proceedings the 'groundlings' began to cheer, whistle, blow motor horns and burst into song now and again. The Junior Dean rushed in and handed out fines right and left, but he was completely ignored, soon gave up and I doubt that the fines were ever collected. To my great surprise the dignitaries on the platform smiled indulgently throughout. Candidates and platform party had a printed list of the names and proposed degrees and the business proceeded without apparent hitch. This strange departure from the quite strict discipline enforced generally has long vanished. When my daughter Anna was conferred with an MSc in 1991, a dignified yet friendly decorum prevailed.

Shortly after graduating from Trinity in 1945, I was invited to join the editorial committee of *Comhar*, an Irish-language monthly first published in 1942 by An Comhchaidreamh, which had been founded in 1935 as an association of the Gaelic Societies in the three colleges of the NUI, with TCD and Queen's College, Belfast. Seán Ó hÉigeartaigh was then Stiúrthóir, Seán MacRéamoinn was Eagarthóir and Máire Mhac an tSaoi and Tomás de Bhaldraithe among the other members.

From then on I became known as Anraí Ó Baoigheallláin to a steadily widening circle of new friends in a lively and pioneering approach to the cause of reviving the language. (Patricia, unfortunately, having been taught by nuns in the North had never been introduced to the 'sweet and kingly tongue'.) But I now had three Christian names, Harry to friends and family, Henry as author and Anraí to Irish speakers. And I prefer Anraí above the others.

Not that having three names was without its own confusions. In pursuit of exports I once travelled first class to New York on board the *SS United States*, courtesy of Cathleen Ní Houlihan. We all received a printed passenger list and my name was given as Anraí Ó Baoigheallláin, just as it appeared on my passport. The second day out, a friendly elderly American businessman asked me had I noticed this strange, foreign-looking name and he 'opined' that the owner was a Persian carpet merchant and that other passengers he had spoken to thought the same. They were on the look-out for this Eastern with the exotic name. Well, carpet merchant or not, I was duly invited by the Captain to a cocktail party and later to dine at his table. The Purser would have told him that I was a senior Irish Government official and that was the reason for the Captain's attention. Anyway, no one else mentioned Persian carpet merchants to me during the rest of our passage to New York.

Comhar succeeded beyond the best hopes of its founders and became a significant force in the development of modern literature in Irish, publishing poems, short stories and articles from leading writers, many of whom first appeared in print in its pages. Editorial independence was maintained in the face of attempts in its early years to curb it by veiled threats to withdraw its State subvention. This subvention was first given in 1948 and still continues.

Another positive development at this time was the establishment of the publishing firm Sairséal agus Dill in 1945 by Seán Ó hÉigeartaigh and his wife Bríd Ní Mhaoileoin. This revolutionised the publication of books in Irish, which had until then relied almost exclusively on An Gúm, an unimaginative and conservative Government agency. Seán, a Trinity Scholar, had joined the Civil Service on graduation and rose rapidly to the rank of Principal Officer in the Department of Finance. Bríd was also a Trinity graduate. A whole generation of writers found new hope in the encouragement and understanding they received from Sairséal agus Dill. This was then in the future, as was Seán's sudden and untimely death in 1967, a grievous blow to his wife, family and friends.

In 1953 An Comhcaidreamh sponsored another remarkable development, the founding of Gael Linn to promote cultural activities through Irish. A list of the pioneering activities, from drama to film, of this organisation—happily still flourishing—speaks for itself. I was involved from the beginning, in a voluntary capacity, and was an active committee member for many years. Gael Linn's activities were funded through a football pool, based on GAA games, a stroke of genius, the brain child of Dónal Ó Móráin, Ceannasaí. Agents throughout the country and further afield tapped the widespread goodwill towards the language and the countrywide interest in, and support for, GAA games. This ensured the success of the operation from the beginning. Under the dynamic direction of Dónal Ó Móráin, backed up by Riobard MacGoráin and a devoted staff, the funds generated were used to promote many cultural developments that soon won a large and faithful following. A succession of plays in Irish was produced in the Damer Theatre, St Stephen's Green, including the first production of *An Giall*, by Brendan Behan. A later English version, *The Hostage*, produced by Joan Littlewood in London, was a runaway success. Combining melodrama, farce, fantasy and ballad opera, it bore little resemblance to the moving and simple Irish original.

Gael Linn regularly issued records made by the foremost exponents of Irish music and song, produced a newsreel in Irish, shown in cinemas countrywide and made the films *Mise Éire* and *Saoirse*, produced by George Morrison, which introduced the music of Seán Ó Riada to a new audience. A series of light-hearted films, produced by Louis Marcus, featured among others Christy Ring, the famous Cork hurler, and in *Capallology*, a quizzical look at the world of horse lovers.

Gael Linn was only six months in being when it started to broadcast a weekly sponsored programme on Radio Éireann which continued for twenty-seven years until sponsored programmes were dropped by RE. The first announcer was Pádraic Ó Raghallaigh from Galway. His mellifluous voice and soft-spoken Connemara Irish held his listeners under a spell for ten years. The results of the football pools were announced and the public was kept informed of Gael Linn activities. The interest of the listeners in Irish songs and traditional music was fostered in these programmes. Intensive courses in spoken Irish were offered by Foras na Gaeilge, a branch of Gael Linn, and thousands have availed themselves of this service which gave them the confidence to enjoy Irish-speaking company and hold their own there.

In those pre-television days, film-going was the principal leisure activity of the people; it was claimed by the trade that a million went to the pictures weekly and, of course, all the films were imported. Rank Films were persuaded by Gael Linn to accept a 3-minute film *Amharc Éireann* ('This is Ireland') for monthly and then fortnightly showing. A later development was Slógadh, a hosting for school children who came from all parts of the country to compete for prizes in dancing, singing, debating and solo and group instrumental music.

A Television Commission was established by the Government in the 1950s when it became clear that this powerful new medium of communication was here to stay, and that a decision must be made on how it should be established to serve the best interests of the people. Disquieting rumours surfaced that attempts were being made to convince the Government that a small country like Ireland would not have the resources to establish and run a TV service and that the best course would be to license a British service. This thinking, involving the surrender of control of the national identity to a greater or less degree, was totally repugnant to nationalist feeling and Gael Linn was spurred to action. With the help of Irish experts, a plan was prepared for the establishment of an independent service and submitted to the Commission. The technical and financial aspects of the plan had been fully researched, to the extent that NBC America had no hesitation in confirming its viability when later asked to advise.

Once Gael Linn had made this weighty submission, the Government were left with only two possible political decisions, to accept it or set up a State service. They chose the latter and Telefís Éireann was launched on 31 December 1961. Non-Irish appointments were made to the three principal posts, Director, Head of Programmes and Chief Engineer. Looking back on the history of Telefís Éireann since 1961, and leaving aside questions of culture and the language, Gael Linn remains convinced that it would have been far better for the country had the plan proposed by them been adopted with its flexibility and encouragement of resourcefulness.

Becoming involved in Gael Linn's activities introduced me to a world far removed from the popular view of Irish speakers as dull, earnest, fanatical and humourless. This misconception was based partly on prejudice and not supported by any real acquaintance with the world of the 'Gaeilgeorí'. I found Gael Linn people lively, stimulating, irreverent, innovative and exuberant. At parties there always seemed to be plenty of singers with an inexhaustible repertoire, songs mournful, merry, sad and bawdy by turns. Heated arguments ended not in sundered friendships but with laughter. It was a world of people in their twenties and early thirties to whom nothing seemed impossible. There was an exhilaration in the air, a zest for life and a gaiety of spirit. Looking back fifty years, Seán MacRéamoinn, acknowledging that the magic of those days may have passed, succeeded by a professionalism still based on dedication to the same aims, concedes that youth and all it means has only a term to live. *Ní bhíonn san óige ach seal.* I was involved from the beginning but my working contribution was limited to chairmanship of committee meetings for some years and attendance at the Damer and other public events.

The young men and women behind *Comhar* and Gael Linn had graduated in the early 1930s and early 1940s; numbers attending universities did not reach seven thousand until 1944/45. So it could be said that in their day they were a highly educated, élite group with all the confidence and self-belief that goes with that situation. Is it possible to see in the vigour and confidence which informed the phenomenon that was, and is, Gael Linn, a pre-figuration of the Celtic Tiger?

Interlude: It Is Too Much

For this story, first published in *TCD Miscellany* Hilary 1942, I took the pen-name 'Noblai'.

Serge Soniavitch lives in a hut on the steppes with his wife and his daughter Sonia.

It is dawn. Sonia rises and goes to the door. She gazes over the steppes. There is nothing to be seen. Sonia shrugs her shoulders.

Her father is awake now. He groans. 'Have we any vodka?' he asks. Sonia shakes her head. He groans again.

There is a knock at the door. Ivan Ivanovitch enters. He is in love with Sonia. He does not know why. She does not know why. We do not know why.

He sits at the table opposite her. 'You love me?' he asks intensely. She shakes her head. He gazes at her with hungry despair. 'Is there any vodka?' She shakes her head. He groans and beats his forehead on the table. Sonia speaks. 'Do not beat your forehead on the table. We have no other table.' Ivan rises. 'It is too much.' He goes out.

Later a noise like thunder far-off is heard. Sonia stares at Serge. Serge stares at Sonia. 'The Cossacks. Quick.' She shakes her head. 'It is no good. This is Russia. Little father, what can we do.' 'Little daughter, you are a fool. You sent Ivan Ivanovitch away. He has a droshky and horses. I should beat you. But why should I worry. The Cossacks will beat you anyway.' She looks at the floor. Then she raises her heavy eyelids to reproach him. It is too much. They are too heavy. She drops them.

The Cossacks gallop up. All is noise and confusion. Harness jingles, horses snort, Cossacks cuss. They call for vodka. There is none. Their leader curses again. 'It is too much. Burn the house down.'

When the hut is in flames, they gallop away. Sonia and Serge stand and look at the flames. Serge sighs. He is puzzled. There is something on his mind. 'I have forgotten something.'

Sonia spreads her hands. 'Little father, we must go to Moscow. Your brother there will do something.'

He beats her. He feels better. 'Little daughter, Ivan Ivanovitch will come when he sees the flames. Ask him to drive us to Moscow.'

A speck appears on the horizon. It grows. It comes nearer. It is Ivan Ivanovitch. He drives a droshky and two horses. Who would expect it? Enough, it is Russia.

Serge salutes him. He kisses him on both cheeks. He signs to Sonia. Sonia kisses him on both cheeks. Ivan is overcome.

He points at the ruins of the hut, 'The Cossacks?' They nod. He grinds his teeth. It is too much. The horses try to bolt.

Serge gives Sonia a hint to speak. She rubs her ankle and speaks quickly. 'Ivan, we go to my uncle in Moscow. You love me? You will follow me?' 'To the ends of the earth.'

Sonia enters the droshky. Serge enters the droshky. Serge speaks. 'Ivan, I think you should follow Sonia now.' Ivan bows. Ivan enters the droshky. They set off for Moscow.

They have gone only twenty kilometres, when Sonia speaks. 'Little father, you are troubled. Speak.' Serge speaks. 'I have forgotten something.' Ivan exclaims. 'Where is the little mother?'

'Ah, that is it.' Serge shrugs his houlders. 'I knew I had forgotten something. She is still in the house.'

They drive on. It is very cold. Suddenly, howling is heard. Wolves. The howling comes nearer. Ivan speaks. 'Little father, the wolves are hungry. I must follow Sonia to Moscow.' He pushes Serge out of the droshky. He bows to Sonia. 'Your father is a brave man.'

Sonia stares at him. She is very cold. He is very stupid. He forgot to take off Serge's fur coat. Cold fury seizes her. She pushes Ivan out of the droshky.

Sonia drives on. She is still cold. Stupid. She did not take off Ivan's fur coat. It is too much. She pushes herself out of the droshky.

The steppes are silent in the dark night.

6 Promoting Gaeltacht Industries

In 1947 I was promoted to the Gaeltacht Services Division section of the Department of Lands, as Assistant Director, and in 1952 became Director. This Division was a direct descendant of the Congested Districts Board, probably the most successful of the innumerable Boards set up in the last fifty years of British rule. It arose out of the Gaeltacht Commission established by General Mulcahy in the Cumann na nGaedheal Government during the 1920s. It eventually came to rest in the Department of Lands with the general object of providing an economic basis for the survival of the Gaeltacht and the native Irish-speaking population.

Despite sixty years of State attention, the people were still very impoverished. I remember driving down a boreen in West Connemara and being held up briefly by two teenage boys driving cattle back to pasture after milking. As they saluted me with a wave and a grin in passing I was struck by their lively expressions, with the eyes in their heads fairly dancing with intelligence. As I drove on, I thought: 'What chance in life have they? There's nothing for them at home. It's the emigrant ship and take their chances in America, or England and a pick-and-shovel with MacAlpine's Fusiliers.' That day is gone, thank God, and good riddance to it. I'm glad I've lived to see it go. I was told of a boy from a large family being late for school and scolded for this by the teacher in front of the class. The boy shifted from foot to foot at this humiliation and finally burst out: 'Had I a spoon, had I?'—he had had to wait his turn for the family spoon.

The Gaeltacht areas were then the back of beyond. Roads were dreadful, full of potholes. In Connemara the road was built on a bog and had a permanent wave—if you attempted any speed at all, it would shake your car to bits. The rural electrification scheme had not reached that far. Streets were unlit, a Tilly oil lamp hissed at you in your room. The experienced traveller always carried a torch. Unemployment was rampant and literally hundreds of young emigrants jumped at any chance of returning to employment at home. In the Division's spinning mill in Kilcar, where wool straight from the sheep's back was turned into yarn of varying strength, I once met a weaver who had just delivered a web of cloth which he had carried on his back the five miles from his house in the mountains. The web was no light load, a length of 75 yards could weigh 4–5 stone. With part of the payment he bought a donkey. He slapped its rump and said, 'You'll carry the load from now on, not me any more.' By the way, a donkey supplied by the Congested Districts Board was always called 'the congisted ass'.

The areas of Galway, Donegal and Mayo that the Gaeltacht Services were concerned with had a population of some 230,000 of whom over half were recorded as Irish speakers. The specific remit was to develop and maintain local industries such as tweed, knitwear, embroidery and toys. Grants were given to encourage the building of new and better houses. The Division ran factories which gave direct employment throughout Gaeltacht areas from Connemara to Donegal. Several hundreds (mostly women) worked in the two toy factories in Mayo and Donegal, and the spinning mill in Donegal. In addition, about a hundred weavers worked at home in the traditional fashion. The products were marketed under the trading name, Gaeltarra Éireann.

One of the Gaeltacht ventures that gave me great satisfaction was the development of seaweed harvesting and processing with an English company, Alginate Industries Ltd. AIL had been founded just after the Second World War to exploit the potential of alginic acid in seaweed. A young English research chemist called Stanford found himself obliged to emigrate as far as Chile to find a remunerative job. The work turned out to be dull and badly paid. He was far from home, family and friends, and it was a struggle to communicate in a foreign language. He got more and more depressed to the degree that he began to think of suicide. Then a friend lent him a copy of *The Worst Journey in the World*, an account of Captain Robert Scott's expedition to the South Pole by Apsley Cherry-Garrard, a member of the expedition who was not included in the final stage of the attempt on the Pole. Scott reached the Pole only to find that the Norwegian Amundsen had forestalled him. He and his four companions perished on their journey back to their base. Apsley Cherry-Garrard gives a searing account of the hardships endured by all the members of the expedition under extreme Antarctic conditions and how they managed to maintain morale and good spirits throughout. Stanford was so affected by this story of quiet heroism, that he shook off his depression, got down to his work and demonstrated the valuable properties of the alginic acid in certain seaweeds. He also developed a process for the extraction of algin and later this became the basis for Alginate Industries' commercial success.

The commercial exploitation of his scientific work was delayed by two world wars but in 1945 a group of old Etonians recruited by Ralph Merton and his brother William, and backed by the merchant banker Leo d'Erlanger, set up operations in Scotland. Sea rods, or stems of large weed, usually tossed ashore after a storm, had been identified as the most effective source of the alginate. Encouraged by us in Gaeltacht Services, in 1947 when additional supplies were needed to supplement Scottish resources, they built a factory in Kilkieran, Connemara, to process sea rods from Irish harvesters. Under Irish law then, a foreign company could not have majority control of an Irish company. Alginate Industries (Ireland) Ltd was owned 51 per cent by MacDonagh's, the biggest merchants in Galway, suppliers of fertiliser, seeds etc and 49 per cent by AIL. Thirty men were employed at Kilkieran. AIL was still in its early stages, had not yet earned a profit and the Irish company also showed a daunting loss in its first year. Personal relations betweeen the Irish and British sides deteriorated, so it was hardly surprising that MacDonagh's lost faith in the venture. Realising that it would be difficult to find another Irish partner, Alan Stewart, the AIL board member responsible for the Irish end, came to me in Gaeltacht Services. He said that unless the Irish Government came to their rescue and bought MacDonagh's shares they would be obliged to close the Kilkieran factory.

This was a formidable challenge, to persuade Government to enter into partnership with a foreign company, which had so far not earned a profit, admittedly only a short while after its setting up to develop a new product. But the closing of the Irish factory and the loss of thirty jobs in an area of high unemployment would be a huge blow and a disastrous setback to hopes of other initiatives. I thought we should take the positive approach.

Discussions with the AIL Board of Directors in their London headquarters convinced me that their belief in their product was well-founded. Better still I obtained 'a letter of comfort' (the first time I had ever heard of such a thing) from Leo d'Erlanger, their merchant banker. He expressed his complete confidence in the undertaking and backed his view by advancing half a million pounds for working capital.

The next step was to get the approval of the Department of Finance. A very sticky conference seemed about to end in stalemate when T. K. Whitaker said, 'I think we might let Gaeltacht make their case to Government'. Although only in his early thirties, he was already recognised as a coming man; the others listened to him with marked attention and agreed to his proposal. The founder of Gaeltacht Services Division, General Mulcahy, was leader of Fine Gael and an influential member of the Government. His life-long committment to the language and the welfare of the Gaeltacht was well-known. I think that Whitaker knew that he would almost certainly support our project and his own shrewd and perceptive interjection ensured that Mulcahy would at least see it. But when our memo to Government was sent forward, McElligott, the long-serving Secretary of the Department of Finance, heard of the proposal for the first time. He hit the roof. He ordered that a strong counter memo be sent. This reminded me of an often-quoted remark by Sarsfield Hogan, senior Assistant Secretary in Finance, 'The Department of Finance is like an inverted Micawber, waiting for something to turn down.'

Despite this opposition the Government gave us the go-ahead, and I felt sure that this was due to support from General Mulcahy. We thought that was that, all we had to do was buy the Irish-held shares. But Finance had another shot in its locker. It decreed that such an 'unusual' proceeding (Finance-speak for 'totally irresponsible') would require Dáil and Senate approval. (It should be said that this use of seaweed was frankly a bit exotic. Alan Stewart told me that he was once on a train from London to Glasgow when the only other passenger in the compartment, by way of introducing himself, said: 'I'm in steel. What's your line?' Alan replied 'I'm in seaweed.' The other sat back, clearly affronted, and said in a huff: 'Well! If you don't want to tell me what you do, that's alright, but there's no need to be so damned rude about it!') So we had to have legislation prepared, passed by both Houses and signed and promulgated by the President. The Minister of the time, Big Joe Blowick—a twenty stone Mayo man whose country accent hid a sharp perceptive mind—piloted the Bill through the various stages. Joe had a colourful turn of speech. Once when I went to him with an awkward problem, he commented 'that's a thorny stick you have there in your hand, Mr Boylan.'

The whole proposal had taken two strenuous years of effort, 1947 to 1949. After all this it was fortunate for us that the Irish company, renamed Arramara Teo, (Sea Products Ltd), proved a success from the start and I was both relieved and gratified that we had justified Whitaker's decisive interjection. He is a fluent Irish speaker, a strong supporter of Cumann Merriman, and a regular attender at their Summer and Winter Schools. I was Joint Managing Director with Alan Stewart for many years. We had one slack year, after four or five years, and I remember being stunned by a colleague's jealousy as he hissed at me after the bad result became known: 'What are your shares worth now!'

Our job in Arramara was to supply semi-processed weed to Scotland for final processing and sale there. We initially harvested about three thousand tonnes of the weed a year, dried and milled it and then despatched it to Scotland in sacks. In the Kilkieran factory the weed was dried in a steel drum of six feet diameter and about 50 feet length. Inside, flanges projected from the sides of the drum at intervals to keep the weed moving. A man was sent in to clean the drum every Monday morning. This man realised that although there was a clear large notice on the front of the drum warning about starting it revolving while someone was inside, some careless or stupid fool was sure to press the starting button without thought. And it happened, but this man was prepared. He was tall, about six feet and took quick hold of one flange and braced his feet against the opposite side of the drum. Fortunately, the manager happened by before the drum had gathered much speed, and instantly pressed the button from 'On' to 'Off'. The drum slowed down, stopped, the door opened, and the man emerged, shaken but unharmed. His native wit had saved him from severe injury.

One innovation I introduced as Joint Managing Director of the Irish operation, was to propose a source of alginate other than the sea rods, whose supply was dependent on stormy weather (a safe enough bet in the west). Driving along the Connemara coast, I saw that large areas of rock stretching for miles along the shore were covered by a seaweed called locally rockweed. This was *Ascophyllum Nodosum*. We collected some, sent it to Scotland for analysis, and the word came back that it was usable (as many types of seaweed are not for various chemical reasons). The weed was harvested on a four-year cycle at low tide, with sickles. The rockweed added another two thousand tonnes to our annual output.

Our sales agreement with AIL provided the opportunity to make a good profit on steady production to the required standards; indeed, after a few years we began to pay the Government a dividend on their shares, an unheard of proceeding for State companies. For the gatherers, mostly small farmers, whose other income was received at long intervals, the cash paid regularly for seaweed deliveries was very welcome.

The Kilkieran factory was run by Don Robb, who had worked in the Scottish factory. I looked after the financial end and the liaising with the Government, Alan Stewart, Joint Managing Director in the AIL side, looked after the factory end. From the start the partnership worked very well.

After I had become a director in 1949, I visited London regularly to confer with AIL and got to know their directors and banker, Leo d'Erlanger. They were both challenging and stimulating in business dealings and very good company over a meal afterwards. Educated at Eton and either Oxford or Cambridge, they ran their business with exceptional efficiency and energy and I learned a great deal as they applied their skills in the management of Arramara. And above all, their word was their bond. They drove a hard but fair bargain and honoured it in spirit and letter. To them, there was only one school, Eton. They did not care about, nor had they any interest in, any other school you might have attended. I remember lunches in d'Erlanger's merchant bank, where we sat at a large round table and helped ourselves from a side table as the servants had taken themselves

off as soon as they had seen that we had everything we wanted. The
talk of the Bank seniors and AIL directors was a real window into
big business and financial London and I'm sure that had I money to
invest, I could have benefited from many valuable tips.

Like the AIL directors, d'Erlanger, a French aristocrat, was an
old Etonian, had served in France in the Second World War and
then joined the family bank 'starting with the inkpots'. With the
family banking genius, he had a flair for identifying and financing
young industrial pioneers. AIL benefited from this gift. He had also
been involved in the formation of the pioneering British Airways.
His father was godson of Pope Leo XIII, (hence the Christian name),
an authority on Arab music, and was architect of 'an entrancing
Arab palace', he built for himself in Sidi-bou-Said in Tunisia (it is
now on public view to tourists). Leo had inherited this treasure; it
was said that the only time Leo showed any interest in the progress
of the Second World War was when there seemed a danger that
Rommel's Afrika Korps would billet in the palace. A man of great
charm, tall, handsome and elegant in the understated French manner,
he appreciated the importance of Arramara's contribution to AIL's
operations and did not fail to assure me from time to time of his
continuing support. He attended Mass in Farm Street every morning
on his way to the City, 'paying his respects to his Maker before taking
on Mammon', as Alan Stewart said. He was a strong backer of the
Channel Tunnel project but died before it became a reality.

Irish business had then few firms engaged in high technology
industry. Wholesale and retail merchandising, banking and insurance
on traditional lines, and a predominance of family ownership,
constituted the Irish scene. The proverbial 'yard of counter' was the
path to prosperity. The Irish Management Institute had not yet
appeared. AIL brought to Arramara strict budgeting and control of
cash-flow. Each week I received a report showing production and
cost against budget, and samples of the product were sent to AIL for

analysis. Sharp questioning followed on any short-fall in quality and my opposite number, Alan Stewart, came to Ireland on frequent inspections. And so the partnership flourished. In 1980, thirty years later, a Joint Committee of Dáil and Senate on State-Sponsored Bodies gave their verdict: 'The Joint Committee was impressed by the evidence of Arramara's continuing expansion and profitability over the past thirty years and by the fact that it has met its objective of providing employment in the Gaeltacht areas while continuing to achieve a good financial performance. (Signed, Senator Eoin Ryan, Chairman)'. A gratuitous and misleading 'submission' was made by the Department of the Gaeltacht to the Committee to inform it that 'a higher level of employment than in Arramara had been attained by several of Gaeltarra's subsidiary and associated companies.' (These companies operated under the aegis of the Department.) The Committee dealt summarily with this contribution. 'The Joint Committee feels that it should be borne in mind that in addition to direct employment, Arramara provides indirect employment for collectors of seaweed.' In a total of £538,000 paid in wages and to gatherers in 1978, over £500,000 was paid to gatherers. It is difficult to understand why the Department should seek to belittle the outstanding success of a Gaeltacht company.

In 1968 Arramara opened a second factory at Meenmore, Dungloe, Co. Donegal. At the dinner following the opening I called on Seosamh Mac an Iomaire, Joe Ridge of our Connemara staff, who had won many awards for singing at the Oireachtas. He gave us *'Níl sé 'na Lá'*, a drinking song with a catchy chorus, well known to many of the locals, who joined in with a will. To shouts of *'Croc suas é, Neidín'*, one of them, another fine singer, gave us *'Preab san Ól'* and our Alginate friends raised their glasses to the company at the chorus like the rest of us. It was a new experience for them, the most enjoyable 'formal', or 'official' dinner they had ever been at, and they were very taken with it.

Séamus MacGarvey, a native of Dungloe, having served his time as an apprentice carpenter, could find no employment at home and went off to Scotland. Shortly after, he heard of the setting up of the Arramara factory, came home, and approached Leslie Hyde, newly appointed manager. Leslie was a very good judge of men, and he at once took Seamus on as a tractor driver. Before long he was foreman and when Leslie retired seven or eight years later, he strongly recommended Seamus to succeed him. The board had no difficulty in agreeing. Séamus MacGarvey is today a very successful Chief Executive of Arramara and has guided its fortunes with great ability, being exceptionally good at staff relations.

It was a great pleasure to meet him again in 1997 at a dinner in Uachtar Ard to celebrate the company's 50th year in operation. Each guest received a crystal paper weight made at Falcarragh, Co. Donegal, embodying a new company logo. When I congratulated Séamus on the logo, he told me that he had organised a competition for a design among secondary schools along the weed-harvesting coasts from Malin Head in Donegal to Loop Head in Clare. The prize was won by two girls from Scoil Phobal MhicDara, Carna, Connemara, Veronica Lydon, Letter Ard, West Cashel and Catherine Corbett, Carna.

Arramara depends on the gatherers for supply of raw material and as well as producing the attractive logo the competition evoked great interest among the families and goodwill towards Arramara. It was typical of Séamus's flair to initiate this plan which pleased so many and obviated employing an expensive agency. And school children do not lack imagination and creative ability.

We donated a cup for competition at Kilkieran Regatta and I duly attended to present it. There were races for currachs and for sail boats, hookers and the smaller gleoiteóg and púcán. The starter stood up in a currach about 100 yards off the pier head and after sundry shouts and exhortations to muster the competitors into line, fired a shotgun to start them. The pier was crowded and the trophies were displayed on a table on the open flat back of a lorry. Stiofán Ó Faharta in his swift *gleoiteóg* beat a yacht from Clifden into second place to local delight. He had taken me out for a sail in the bay several times and I can still hear him shout '*Scaoil amach a' jib*' as I tended the jib sheets.

I was a Director of Arramara for thirty-three years, serving as Joint Managing Director for some twenty years and then as Chairman until my resignation in 1982. The previous year AIL had been taken over by Merck, an international American company, with the result that the two English Directors had been replaced by Americans. I did not find them agreeable to work with, I missed my old friends from AIL and after a robust altercation over severance pay for some workers (which I won) and accusations that I had exceeded my authority and had been far too generous—on the lines of 'We was robbed'—I decided to call it a day.

Shortly before our next Board meeting, we received a letter from Merck, informing us that their company policy required them to have complete control of their associated companies. Accordingly, they proposed to sell their minority share holding in Arramara. Our shareholder, the Minister for the Gaeltacht, then Máire Geoghegan-Quinn, was told immediately of this development and reminded that as Arramara was incorporated as a private limited company, our Articles laid down that no shares could be sold without the consent of the Directors and that we had a majority on the Board. To my great satisfaction, the Minister said instantly, 'Refuse permission to sell.' When we convened for the next Board meeting, it gave me wicked pleasure to convey this decision to the Merck Directors. I savoured their fury and discomfiture at the realisation that they were 'locked in'. At the end of the meeting I announced my resignation. We were equally glad to see the backs of each other.

Alan Stewart became a good friend and stayed with us on visits to Dublin. Over six feet tall, he closely resembled the film star Rex Harrison, for whom he was often taken. He had worked as a young 'second' in Bumpus's a leading London book shop and was very well read. He was married for seventeen years to Audrey Withers, editor of British *Vogue* from 1940 to 1960, so the London fashion and journalist worlds were well represented at parties in their house in Little Venice. They divorced, amicably, when Audrey, returning from a business trip to New York, met an old friend—a Russian horologist—on shipboard. They fell in love all over again. Married after the divorce, Audrey retired from *Vogue* and according to report they were blissfully happy in a remote country house which echoed all day to the chiming of the innumerable clocks of her new husband. She died in October 2001 at the age of ninety-six.

Alan gave me a wry account of how 'evidence' of his 'adultery' was put together to meet the stringent legal requirements for divorce at the time. There were specialised agencies to make the discreet but sufficient arrangements. Following instructions Alan took the afternoon train to Brighton, known as 'the Flying Fornicator', and met a middle-aged Mrs John Smith by arrangement. Rooms had been booked for them and after a tedious dinner they retired to these adjoining rooms. At 8 am Alan rang for morning tea and knocked on the communicating door to Mrs Smith's room. She emerged wearing a nightdress that reached from her chin to her toes and got into bed beside Alan. A maid arrived with the tea and having been duly primed took a good look at the 'guilty pair'. She had barely closed the door behind her when Mrs Smith was out of the bed like a flash and back to her room, closing and locking the door behind her. It was the last Alan ever saw of her.

Within two years, Alan married again and with his new wife, Noëlle, came on a holiday to stay with us in a house in Carraroe which we had rented that summer. Noëlle was Australian, a 'fine figure of a woman', and much younger than Alan. Like most Australians, she loved the outdoors and went swimming every day. One morning when I came down to the kitchen, she was there before me, in her bikini, ready for the sea. Just then, there was a knock at the door and before I could move, Noëlle skipped over to open it. When I got there I saw it was Seán the Post. His eyes were 'out on sticks', looking at Noëlle in her well-filled bikini. He turned to me and said with a knowing look, '*Tá sí féin sportúil,*' (Herself is a sporting woman). Perhaps she was too sporting for her elderly new husband, for the marriage came to an end shortly after.

Alan's third and last wife, Valerie, was the daughter of the Secretary of the Royal Society, who had survived four years as an infantry officer in the First World War. He was so grateful for being alive that he spent his time when home reading a book a day. Augustus John was a friend and Valerie modelled for him and being a big, strong young woman was able to defend herself from his amorous advances, a necessary talent for any woman modelling for John. Alan became a father for the first time in his life at sixty and became at once completely absorbed in his daughter Sophie. But within a few years he died of a heart attack. I travelled down from London with AIL Director Freddie Griffith-Jones to the funeral in Fordingbridge, Hampshire. It was a cremation and as we drove through the entrance gates, we saw a large notice board listing the names and times for the day's proceedings. Freddie was horrified. 'Do you see that? My God, it's like a race card. I see that Alan is down to go in the 2.30.' And when we set out for London later, Freddie said with great fervour, 'I'll have none of that carry-on. I want to be buried properly like a Christian.'

Quite soon after Arramara was established, the first President of Ireland, Dr Douglas Hyde died. Since he was a Protestant, his funeral service was held in St Patrick's Cathedral. At that time, Catholics were forbidden to attend non-Catholic services and so during the service members of the Government waited outside the Cathedral. This moved Austin Clarke to write a satirical poem 'Burial of an Irish President'.

> *Costello, his Cabinet,*
> *In Government cars, hiding*
> *Around the corner, ready*
> *Tall hat in hand, dreading*
> *Our Father in English. Better*
> *Not hear that 'which' for 'who'*
> *And risk eternal doom.*

Some English newspapers commented on this, to them, inexplicable behaviour and Alan was curious to hear my version. I told him, 'Yes, that's the rule laid down by the Church, Catholics may not attend a Protestant service.' He said, 'What about the burial? Could you go to the cemetery?'

I told him what I believed to be the Church instruction. 'You may go to the cemetery, but you should stand apart and show by your demeanour that you are not taking any part in the ceremony.'

'So what would you do then? Whistle a jig?'

I am sure that, back in 'Pagan England', Alan dined out more than once on that story.

I remember another occasion in Fordingbridge when we had dinner with friends of Alan. The guests included Nicolette Devas and her second husband, a painter, Rupert Shepherd, a big, burly man known as Rupert the Bear, Alan with his third wife, Valerie and myself with my first (and only) wife, Patricia.

Nicolette was a daughter of Francis MacNamara of Ennistymon House, Co. Clare. Her first husband, Anthony Devas, a successful portrait painter, had died after 27 years of marriage. Her sister, Caitlín was married to the Welsh poet, Dylan Thomas. Francis had abandoned his wife and family seven years after marriage for a serie of liaisons and his wife moved to Hampshire, near Fordingbridge. The children were brought up with the neighbouring family of Augustus John. In 1966 Nicolette had published *Two Flamboyant Fathers*, a vivid and astringent account of her life in Co. Clare as a child and on later extended visits and her upbringing with the Augustus Johns. Patricia was responding to a remark by her when Nicolette interjected waspishly, 'Don't you put words into my mouth or I shall ROUGH UP.' It was a brief encounter that could have come straight from her book. Later in the evening when the brandy had circulated, everyone seemed in a mellow mood and there was philosophising and the exchange of deep or perhaps very shallow thoughts masquerading as profound. I found myself sitting beside Nicolette. She insisted that she was the square one of her Bohemian family, but after some desultory exchanges she suddenly fixed me with her penetrating gaze and said, 'There are times in a woman's life when she needs to be hugged and caressed, kissed and f—ed.' And so the evening went.

We met again in London some ten years later at a party given by Souzelle de la Maisoneuve, an exotic Frenchwoman who ran the Chastenet European Art Centre, a gallery in Seymour Place, an establishment funded by Swiss bankers. On a visit to Dublin she had called on us and seen some of our eldest son, Hugo's paintings. She greatly admired his work and arranged an exhibition in her gallery. It was well received, a welcome encouragement to a young artist. Nicolette had aged, but her gaze remained as sharp as ever. This time she contented herself by merely saying that she delighted in sex and the savour it gave to life and loving, while smiling at Rupert the Bear. Souzelle herself had been married three times and when I asked her whether she ever thought of marrying again she exclaimed vehemently *Jamais! Jamais plus!* The Swiss bankers apparently got tired, either of supporting art or of Souzelle, for we next heard that she was back in France as public relations officer for a château that had been turned into a hotel. She sent us a pressing invitation but we were not able to avail ourselves of it for various reasons. On her next appearance in Dublin she created a stir at a party when drinks were being offered, exclaiming, 'Champagne for Patricia. Patricia never drinks anything but champagne.'

Among the directors of Alginates was Charlie Cameron, younger son of the Laird of Lochiel. The Clan Cameron supported the Young Pretender, Bonny Prince Charlie in 1745 and this cost them dearly after the defeat of the Highlanders at Culloden. Charlie joined the Cameron Highlanders in 1939 straight from school and fought against Rommel in the desert. He was twice blown up, was lost in the desert for nearly a week and his fellow officers were so glad to see him again that they saw to it that he was awarded the Military Cross his bravery deserved. After the war, he joined Alginate Industries and made many visits to Ireland. When airports first installed metal detectors following gun scares, Charlie activated one at Heathrow. He was sent through again with the same result, told to empty his pockets and finally taken away for a rigorous search. Nothing suspicious was found and the security men reluctantly allowed him to board the aircraft. The problem was that the surgeon who had operated on him to remove from his back the shrapnel lodged there when he was blown up had told him, 'I'm leaving a few small pieces, I've carved you up enough and these won't do you any harm.' On return home, Charlie went to his doctor, related this experience and procured a suitable certificate, which both astonished and satisfied airport security staff.

Interlude: Barnabas

This was first published under my own name in the *Irish Press* 4 January 1947.

Brother Barnabas was sad. He knew why but could see no way of removing the cause. He was ploughing the bottom field this harsh March day. Other days, the sight of the black earth starting away from the bite of the coulter gave him pleasure. Other days he whistled and encouraged his horse with exclamations and shouts. The shaggy-fetlocked animal liked to hear his voice and butted his strong shoulders into the wind and up the slope as if making little of the labour.

He knew that Oisín ploughed better for being praised. He whinnied when they gained the headland and Barnabas looked back on the straight, clean furrow. When he faced him down the hill, the little lay brother could give him only a half-hearted 'Up there, Oisín! Up, Boy.' The wind whooped at them in sudden forays, pressing his rough woollen habit against his body and then retreating behind the copse of beech trees that guarded the monastery buildings. He tried not to think of the work going forward there.

Brother Ciarán would be busy at his new Gospel, his face bent over the vellum. Every monk or abbot or bishop or prince who came the way asked, as soon as decency permitted, to see Ciarán's manuscript. Tag-ends of praise from the visitor would reach Barnabas, sitting at the lower end of the refectory table. And in the foundry, Brother Canice was even now casting a new bell. Barnabas had helped, for strong arms were needed to carry in loads of wood charcoal for the furnace and bucket after bucket of water to fill the trough. He had hoped to be allowed to help in the actual casting but even to himself the hope had been faint. The new novice would be there, eager with his quick hands and quicker brain. Barnabas looked at his own strong, square hands, sure on the plough. Soon the new bell would sound over the countryside, compelling as the Spring, 'bidding men cast off the Winter of sin and come to the green pastures of grace,' as the Abbot had said in his homily last Sunday.

Barnabas had thought once that he might find a place with the brush-maker and spend his days plucking and polishing hog bristles, binding them and fitting the base to a cunningly-shaped handle and securing it with bands of tin. But he had unthinkingly whittled all the twigs to the same length and bound them so tightly that, as Brother Brushmaker had said 'it would sweep no better and no worse with the head than with the handle.'

So Barnabas had gone back to the stables and spent his days pulling and hauling like any farmhand. 'Better to have stayed on at my father's poor place in Inishcultra,' he thought.

He swung the ploughshare around as Oisín planted his hooves on the headland. Memories of Inishcultra came to him as he stood looking back over the field. His father had looked troubled when he broached his desire to go to Durrow. 'Have you the learning for it?' he asked.

'If I haven't the head I've the hands,' he had answered with bright confidence. 'They do everything themselves, I'm told, and they will find something for me, never fear.' So he had set out seven years before, but all that the monks of windy Durrow could find for him was ploughing and harrowing, ditching and draining. Better to be back in Inishcultra. He could say his prayers there just as well as here, and at nightfall, instead of a cold, lonely cell, there would be the turf fire and the old men telling stories of Cuchulain and the Fianna. He had tried it for seven years now. 'A long enough apprenticeship and no trade at the end of it,' he thought.

The habit of obedience made him move to the plough, and they

went down the field again, horse and man moving in a slow rhythmic
unison.

'God bless the work.'

He turned at the voice. A monk it was who had saluted him, a small
man like himself, his habit looped up for walking, spatters of mud on
his bare ankles and raw leather sandals.

'May you thrive, too,' he answered. The other looked up the field,
appraising the work.

'Your Abbot has a good ploughman.'

'They're not scarce in Ireland, good ploughmen.'

The monastery bell pealed, calling the monks to Vespers.

'Your Abbot has a good maker of bells. Two good craftsmen.'

'Aye, but good bell-makers are not found in every parish.'

The other moved to the plough and gripped it with his small, brown
hands, feeling it, moving it a little, like a warrior testing a new spear.
He put his hands on Oisín's head and the horse rubbed his nostrils against
the hand and whinnied.

'You'll be unyoking him now. I'll give you a hand.'

Barnabas forgot his sadness as they worked together. 'Are you for
Durrow?'

'I am, I'll walk up with you.'

They walked together in silence for a while, then the stranger spoke
again.

'The best ploughman I ever knew told me that none but happy men
could plough straight and true because to do so they must be straight
and true themselves and that means that they are happy.'

'I'm happy when I'm ploughing, except—'

He stopped, abashed at the sound of his own voice and at what he
was saying.

'Except? Speak, my son.'

'Except when I think of Brother Ciarán and Brother Canice
illuminating manuscripts and casting bells and everybody praises their
work, and, and. . .'

'Go on, my son.'

Barnabas drew a quick breath. How easy it was to talk to this man!

'And I'm no good at any of these things. I can only clean stables and milk and plough. I'm doing just the same work as if I had stayed at home.'

They walked along, again in silence, save for the rustle of their habits and the sound of Oisín's hooves on the path.

'Was your ploughman a monk?'

'He was a bishop.'

They had come nearer to the monastery and the path divided. The stranger turned to Barnabas. 'You will be going that way to the stables. God go with you.'

He raised his hand in blessing and turned towards the oratory. Barnabas clumped over to the stables. As he fed and watered Oisín his mind was on the words of the stranger monk. A bishop who ploughed and was happy! He could not understand. There it was again, he wasn't really suited to this world of people who could work so well with their hands and also understand hard passages in the Scriptures and the writings of the Fathers. Maybe old Father John could explain to him what the stranger had meant.

He was ready for supper when he shuffled into the refectory. Hunger shot his eyes to the long table, although he knew that the meal would be the same as always, a small loaf of bread and a measure of milk for each. Grace said, he sat down and fell to. While they ate, a novice read from St Paul's Epistles. He finished quickly and sat quietly, trying to stifle the wish that the meal had been larger.

The novice read on:

'For it is written in the law of Moses, Thou shalt not muzzle the mouth of the ox that treadeth out the corn. Doth God take care for oxen? Or sayeth He it altogether for our sakes? For our sakes no doubt this is written: that he that plougheth should plough in hope; and he that plougheth in hope should be partaker of his hope.'

There was a sudden silence. Barnabas was grappling with the words of Paul. 'He that plougheth should plough in hope.' They seemed to echo what the stranger monk had said about ploughing and being happy. If he could only understand these sayings, maybe he could content himself here.

That was their Abbot speaking now. There was a sudden stir of interest among the cowled heads. They all seemed to turn at the same time to the top of the table.

'The founder of this our house desires to speak a few words to his brothers in Jesus Christ.'

Colmcille! Colmcille! The name was on every lip. Barnabas lowered his eyes. It was enough for a lay brother to listen when this man of noble blood, prince of the Church and poet, spoke. After the first few words he looked up, startled. It was the voice of the stranger monk who had said to him, 'Speak, my son.' The words, at first, he did not grasp. Then, in the stillness, they came home to him. Colmcille spoke of the life of the soul, of prayer and fasting and night-watching. He spoke of grace to fight the good fight, of Faith, Hope and Charity, 'and the greatest of these is Charity.' He spoke of work, of labouring with the hands for the greater glory of God. Here he paused and Barnabas had a strange feeling that he was speaking directly to him.

'My brothers, use ye your talents as God gave them to ye. To one, to copy manuscripts, to another, to make shrines for his altars, to another, to cast bells to call his people to prayer. And in the field, let him who works there remember the words of Paul, "He that plougheth should plough in hope. He, too, will have a mansion in Heaven."'

Barnabas rose with the others and followed along the corridors to the oratory. In the wide sleeves of his habit, his hands were locked together, bunching the muscles of his forearms. Prayer now, and then to his cell. He would sleep well, for tomorrow he could go ploughing again, ploughing in hope as his master Colmcille had taught him.

7 Putting Donegal Tweed on the Map

Donegal hand-woven tweed had always been popular for both men's and women's clothing. On our staff we had a tweed designer of genius called Jim Redington. He had been appointed Assistant Manager of the industries, but it quickly became obvious that his real talent was in the creation of subtle and colourful tweeds. He envisaged the colours, perhaps dyeing the yarn in our spinning factory, and the weavers produced swatches, large patterns which our agents would then use to market our tweeds, mainly abroad. At the time Harris tweeds from the Hebrides were extremely well-known, and our task was to try to create a similar 'brand' for Donegal tweed. I was soon convinced that the beautiful cloths produced on hand-looms by Donegal weavers to Redington's designs were equal, if not superior, to the world-famous Harris tweeds from the Hebrides. The Harris tweeds were designed for sporting wear, rather check-like, square, whereas the tweeds that he designed were softer and gently colourful. Sales of the Donegal tweeds were laughably small in comparison with the Harris brand and I saw no reason why this should not be changed.

We thought that if big names in the fashion world could be enlisted on our side, and Donegal tweed promoted properly, it was bound to sell. Accompanied by Jim Redington, I travelled widely in the 1950s, and we appointed agents in France, Germany, Italy and Spain. Visits to England and the United States followed to put agents already there 'in the picture'. The next step was to interest a leading figure in the burgeoning Irish fashion industry in our product. Sybil

Connolly immediately came to mind and needed little persuasion to use our tweeds in her collections. She had already made Irish crochet known and admired and was quick to see and appreciate the attraction of this new lightweight tweed. Donegal tweeds got a further boost when Patricia interviewed her for Radio Éireann.

Then to the English market. Through Audrey Withers, Alan Stewart's wife, I secured an introduction to Hardy (later Sir Hardy) Amies, couturier to the Queen. We lunched together and he was clearly much taken by the swatches of Redington's designs I showed him later in his workrooms. He had not seen such tweeds before, so light yet so firm, in shades evocative of the shifting colours of the Donegal landscape. His interest was not feigned; his next collection included a coat and dress in Donegal tweed. Had we spent thousands on lavish advertising it would not have had a fraction of the value of that endorsement—money could not have bought it.

Our approach soon paid dividends. Orders flowed in from Ireland and increasingly from the US, the UK and France. Of course we were lucky that our timing coincided with the beginning of recovery from the war, and people had the time and money to take an interest in what we were offering. We recruited numbers of weavers, some to start working again at looms long standing idle, others to start afresh, learning from fathers or brothers and quick learners they proved to be. We built a weaving shed in Glencolumcille and provided looms, centre light and space for the weavers we needed to meet the new orders—not all of them would have accommodation for a loom in their small cottages.

All this activity was done within Civil Service rules and practices, developed to serve a parliamentary system of government, but a severe handicap on commercial activities. I remember one trip to the US in which my expenses allowance would have been barely enough for a room in a moderate hotel, when I was trying to sell tweed to the US fashion houses. Luckily Tim O'Driscoll, then

Chairman of Corás Tráchtála, intervened and got me a conference rate from the Department of Finance, which covered a first-class hotel plus a moderate daily allowance. Another limitation was on travel outside Ireland—I could not send someone to London without sanction from the Department of Finance, which could take several weeks to come through.

I astonished myself by silencing the redoubtable John A. Costello, Senior Counsel and Taoiseach in the second Coalition of 1954–7. The 1956 Budget was being prepared and all Departments had sent in their Estimates. These were pared down rigorously by Finance, but still the figures were dreadful. The economic situation was dire and the Fianna Fáil opposition had been hounding the Government in the Dáil and outside. The Government set up a sub-committee to try to cut the Estimates further in a desperate attempt to save the situation, and heads of Departments were summoned one by one before it. Though not a full Department, Gaeltacht Services Division had a separate vote and I received my call. Costello, Taoiseach and noted formidable cross-examiner as Senior Counsel, was in the chair, flanked by Gerard Sweetman, Minister for Finance. The figures were gone through and I put up a dogged resistance to any further cuts, as the Finance men had, I considered, taken every pound that could be spared and more. After a good half-hour of this stone-walling, Costello was getting somewhat testy at his lack of success and he finally seized on the large sum provided for purchase of wool to be spun into yarn for weaving Donegal tweed. He looked at his Finance brief.

'This is one of your largest items.'

'Yes, we have hundreds of weavers working for us.'

'Your figure is based on an average price of 3s 6d per pound.'

I nodded.

'It would make a substantial reduction if you budgeted for 3s or even 3s 3d.'

I looked straight at him.

'This estimate is based on our experience of the market for years past. The man who could forecast the price of wool 15 months ahead could make a fortune. We do the best we can from our experience.'

Costello gave me a sharp, startled look then turned to Sweetman and nodded. Sweetman nodded in return and Costello turned back to me.

'Thank you, Mr Boylan,' and waved his hand in dismissal.

I was outside the room before I realised just what I had done, and made very quick time back to my office.

The Civil Service in the 1940s and 1950s harboured some strange characters. I remember one man who had secured a very high place at the open competitive examination for Executive Officers. It was a written examination only, with no interviews to test for other qualities. This man was placed ninth overall, and was convinced that this gave him prior right to promotion before those who got lower places. For over forty years he kept by him a copy of the printed booklet issued by the Civil Service Commissioners which gave the marks obtained by each candidate. He brooded over it, and grew increasingly bitter as men who had got much lower places were promoted 'over his head'. He made no secret of his feelings and this obsession certainly did not improve his performance of his duties. He was sufficiently diligent and efficient to succeed in advancing several steps up the promotion ladder in the course of time. When he finally retired, the ritual presentation was made by the head of his branch who had risen quickly above him but figured well behind him in 'the book'. He had 'the book' by him and caused great embarrassment to all present by holding it up and referring sarcastically to 'those who had advanced very rapidly in some mysterious way, he knew not how or why.' To everyone's great relief, he did not give names, but there was no doubt who he had in mind.

He was a sad case.

Structures in the Civil Service were then very rigid. When assigned to a Department on entry, you might very well spend the rest of your career there, filling promotion slots as they became available. Transfer to another Department was very rare as it would impinge on promotion prospects of their staff. Some Departments remained at the same strength for years with the result that openings for promotion were rare, occurring only on the death or retirement of a staff member, which led to a morbid interest in the health of elderly colleagues.

One of the legendary characters in the Land Commission was actor and playwright Sam Waddell, known in the literary world as Rutherford Mayne, author of a dozen plays. We saw him give an electrifying performance in the Abbey Theatre in the title role in Eugene O'Neill's *Emperor Jones*. A civil engineer, he joined the Land Commission, rose to be Chief Inspector and then a Lay Commissioner in the court of the Commission. When he was approaching the normal retiring age of sixty-five, a legal friend told him that there was no retiring age laid down in the Land Act under which he was appointed. Waddell naturally welcomed this advice and proclaimed that he was 'a statutory barnacle'. The Government was in no hurry to introduce an amending Bill solely to oblige his expectant successor fretting in the wings, and waited seven years until some amendments became necessary in the ordinary course of business. These took the bare look off the couple of lines giving Waddell tenure until the age of seventy-two and fixing sixty-five as the retiring age for new appointees. The Act was passed in 1950 and Sam retired that year. The unexpected 'bonus' of seven extra years on full pay seemed to give him a new lease of life for he lived to be eighty-nine. The vacancy was filled by the appointment of the Secretary of the Department, W. F. Nally. We had all savoured this comedy and the Act was quickly christened 'the Nally Act'.

There was a strong belief that promotion should be made in strict order of seniority and when a man was promoted out of turn, it caused great bitterness in those passed over. Superior merit was not admitted. It simply did not count. There were dark murmurs about the man promoted. 'His wife is a second cousin of the Minister's wife', or, 'He comes from the same town or county as the Minister'. Three organisations came under great suspicion—the St Vincent de Paul, the GAA and the 'Knights'—and it was freely alleged that if you joined one of them, you had powerful friends there who would look after you. Many of those 'passed over' developed a chip on the shoulder which did not improve their discharge of their official duties. (As we said at the time, a well-balanced Irishman was one with chips on both shoulders.) Actually, of course, the Secretaries and Assistant Secretaries recommending the appointments had a strong interest in promoting the best people. In my experience, on the few occasions when an appointment looked odd or out of turn, it turned out to have been quite right.

My success at the competition for the post in Radio Éireann, open to the entire Civil Service, had marked me out and my promotion thereafter was rapid. However, when I became Director of Gaeltacht Services there was grudging acceptance that my fluent Irish gave me a special claim. It was even said that I was a native speaker.

Occasionally you had to use a little guile to effect change in the routine. I remember one office I worked in, there were about thirty men at various tables, which over time had become piled high with files, some not-quite-finished-with, others just-getting-round-to, others again I-will-probably-need-to-refer-to. It gave the room a bogus appearance of a very busy staff, battling against a heavy workload. Instead of simply insisting that the files be tidied away, which would have been resisted, I announced that because the accumulation of files on the tables was preventing the cleaners from doing their job, it would be necessary in future for all files to be put away in the available cupboards every night. For the first day or two, the same files were carefully put away and taken out again; gradually, however, fewer and fewer files were taken out every morning, and the camouflage disappeared. It was quite unnecessary anyhow, as they were in fact good workers and I liked to think that after a while they came to appreciate the better dust-free atmosphere.

The job of Director was challenging, stimulating and enjoyable. Not least of the pleasure was in the travel. This was both local and international, the latter including representation at conferences. I got to know well the Gaeltachtaí of Connemara, Mayo and Donegal and to appreciate the contribution made by the workers at their looms, on the factory floor and on windswept beaches, harvesting seaweed. I heard Irish spoken as an ordinary language in daily use and gained a fluency and *blas* which still remain with me.

The commercial activities of Gaeltarra Éireann were severely handicapped by having to work within Civil Service rules and practice developed over many years to serve a parliamentary system of government. Attempts to reform were stymied by lack of political interest, until the second Coalition Government of 1954–7 came into power. General Mulcahy, Chairman of Fine Gael, long noted for his sincere dedication to the revival of the language of the Gaeltacht, obtained Government sanction to set up Gaeltarra Éireann as a state-sponsored body. When Fianna Fáil came into power again in March 1957 action was taken under that sanction and the new Board was established on 1 April 1958.

I was asked to remain to help with the change-over and the recruitment of new staff. I discovered that none of the new directors had any experience of industry, or the promotion of exports, coming from backgrounds of retail and wholesale marketing. I was not impressed and when they decided to advertise for a Managing

Director, I did not apply. I also suspected that the Minister would exercise his prerogative and appoint his own political choice. He did just that and in the event the man appointed lasted little over a year. I was well out of that set-up, particularly as in the meantime I had been caught up in a determined campaign to prove that Gaeltarra Éireann was riddled with incompetence, fraud and corruption.

It started on 19 March 1957 when Patrick Lindsay, on his last day as Minister (Fianna Fáil was about to take office), called me into his office and handed me a letter addressed to Patrick Dooley, the most successful of the three Irish sales agents. The letter dismissed Dooley, against whom the Minister had a personal grudge, on the grounds that he had given excess discounts on knitwear to shopkeepers. Under his contract of service, Dooley was subject to dismissal at six months' notice. He had neither salary nor expenses, and was paid solely by commission on sales and spent his time 'on the road'. He was not a member of my staff in the accepted sense, and had no part or authority in the management.

As he handed me the letter, Lindsay said, 'I hold you personally responsible to see that Dooley gets that today.' I repeated what he had already been told, that Dooley had no authority to give discounts and the accounts system would not pass them. Lindsay brushed that aside, sat back in his chair, and giving me a very hard look, said 'If there is any attempt to re-appoint Dooley, I will have a motion passed by Dáil Éireann for an enquiry into the management of Gaeltarra Éireann. You, Mr Boylan, will go into that enquiry with an unblemished reputation but mud will be thrown and some of it will stick to you.'

A few weeks later, Jack Lynch, Minister for the Gaeltacht in the new Government, reinstated Dooley, stating in the Dáil that after full investigation he could find no grounds for Lindsay's decision. As the Dáil records show, Lindsay challenged this action and put down a series of questions about Dooley's earnings and his business interests other than his Gaeltarra agency, which drew from Deputy C. J. Haughey the exclamation 'When will this personal vendetta come to an end?' Lindsay was evidently preparing his case and I remembered with some unease his remark to me about mud being thrown.

In February 1958, he put down his threatened Motion 'that Dáil Éireann should appoint a Select Committee to enquire into the conduct and management of Gaeltarra Éireann'. In the course of the debate, Michael Moran, a solicitor from Mayo, who had succeeded Jack Lynch as Minister, referred to a row at Christmas 1956 between Lindsay and Dooley in the Railway Hotel, Galway, and said that the dismissal of Dooley was due to personal spleen. In the Dáil a week later, in a dramatic gesture, Lindsay waved two pieces of paper in the air, saying that they gave the names of a Dublin wool merchant and a Gaeltarra staff member, and alleged long-standing fraud in the supply of wool to Gaeltarra. This was the beginning of a series of accusations which were to hang over Gaeltarra and myself and my family for a year and a half.

On hearing of Lindsay's accusation in the Dáil, all Gaeltarra records were immediately impounded on Minister Moran's instructions, and an investigation by the Garda was set up by the Minister for Justice. The debate on Lindsay's Motion was adjourned

While the Garda investigation was in progress a standard surprise inspection once a month found that our head office cashier had embezzled £219. I suspended him, sent him home and reported the offence. He undertook to repay the entire amount and did so two days later. He pleaded with me, pale-faced and shaking, to do the best I could for him. But the rules were strict and guardianship of public money was regarded as in our trust. It was a most unpleasant duty. The Department of Finance took over, secured a Government order of dismissal (he was an established permanent and pensionable officer) and instructed the Chief State Solicitor to prosecute. However, when the case came to court two months later, the State offered no evidence, and the case was dismissed.

Informed by a disgruntled insider, Deputy Lindsay raised the case in the Dáil on 6 May 1958. He said 'This man did not bother converting tweed or knitwear into money. He took the money', and alleged that there was deliberate suppression of evidence which would be damaging to Gaeltarra Éireann. The Minister replied that appeals were made by the ex-cashier's lawyers on compassionate grounds, he had a young family and had got another job which he would lose if a conviction was recorded against him. The money was all paid back long before the prosecution was taken and the Minister for Finance had agreed that evidence would not be given. Lindsay SC said 'the Probation Act would have met the case.' The Minister replied, 'the application of the Probation Act is in fact a conviction. I would not take the line of hounding this unfortunate man.' Even a layman could see that the very title 'Probation of Offenders Act' means that the defendant has become an offender, after conviction.

To prove that troubles come in threes, just at this time the annual audit for 1957/8 (which included stocktaking of tweed, knitwear and toys held in the Dublin depot) showed an apparent discrepancy of several thousand yards of tweed. In ordinary circumstances, the auditors and management would have re-examined the records as there must have been some error or oversight to cause such a huge discrepancy. But in view of the Garda investigation, the auditor understandably reported it immediately to the Comptroller and Auditor General who in turn reported it to the Public Accounts Committee which requested that the Accounting Office, in co-operation with the Auditor General, should make an exhaustive stocktaking of all goods in the depot. The newspapers got wind of this 'scandal' again, through insider information, and startling headlines appeared 'MILES OF TWEED MISSING IN GAELTARRA ÉIREANN.' Around this time I met Joe Blowick, my former Minister, in the street and he greeted me warmly. We shook hands and he referred to the headline. 'What's this about miles of tweed missing? How could that be? There must be double counting,' shaking his head in puzzlement. The investigation by the Accounting Department and the Comptroller and Auditor General, which took nearly two months, disclosed the trade practices of allowing a free yard in each roll or web of approximately 75 yards in a handwoven product and of supplying the trade with large patterns or swatches in aid of marketing; this accounted for the discrepancy. The total cost of production was factored into the sale price. In his reply in June 1959 to the resumed Lindsay Motion Minister Moran stated that this explanation was fully accepted by the Comptroller and Auditor General.

The Garda enquiry into the alleged fraud lasted nine months and included several visits to the tweed mill in Kilcar, Co. Donegal, when many long hours were spent interviewing the manager Kenneth Fricker. Eventually we heard that the results of the enquiry had been presented to the Government who had decided to prosecute Tommy Campbell, managing director of Campbell & Co., a leading Dublin wool merchants who were also a major supplier to Gaeltarra, and the workman in the tweed mill who operated the weighbridge, for collusion to defraud. This was bad news.

When the case began in court, I was instructed to attend. The prosecution was led for the State by Brian Walsh, leading Senior Counsel who later became a judge on the Supreme Court. Brian Walsh opened the State case by giving a detailed account of the operations of Gaeltarra Éireann, explaining that this was only a trade name under which the Gaeltacht Services Division of the Department operated rural industries in the Gaeltacht. The prosecution was therefore being made on behalf of the Minister for the Gaeltacht. The second day was devoted to an account of the procedure laid down for the placing of contracts, the whole business of sealed tenders, placed in a sealed box until due for opening, the rank of senior officers who alone could deal with contracts and so on. In the second week Mr Walsh began an exhaustive recital of the details of contracts made for several years past with Campbell and Co.

Tommy Campbell I knew quite well, principally for his fame as the longest driver of a golf ball in Ireland, although not a big or strong man. He came to me in the lunch break and said he had never even met the weighbridge man, or knew of his existence, let alone colluded with him. And Sergeant Farrell, assistant to Superintendant Wymes in the Garda enquiry, said to me 'This case is going to get nowhere. Don't you think so? There's nothing in it.' This was comforting to some degree, although I thought that perhaps he was just 'drawing me out'.

Then came the shattering news that Kenneth Fricker had committed suicide, drowning himself in a dye vat. He was evidently upset and depressed by the frequent Garda investigations and the resultant malicious gossip. At that stage I had resigned myself to the worst. Brian Walsh, after examining the 'evidence' left to him, refused informations and the case collapsed.

Lindsay's Motion was resumed on 10 June 1959. The Minister, Michael Moran, reported that after investigation of the evidence in respect of Lindsay's charges, the court case had been dropped. He went on to say that Lindsay's unfounded allegations had five results: first, a shocking waste of official time and money; second, a reputable firm was slandered and involved in costs of £7,000 or £8,000; thirdly, an unfortunate man lost his life up in Donegal, leaving a widow and family; fourthly, irreparable damage was done to Gaeltarra Éireann business; fifthly, irreparable damage was done to, and a cloud left over, conscientious civil servants who for many years had served under different governments. Lindsay's Motion was then put to the House. No one had spoken in favour of it except himself and it was ignominiously defeated.

As to the embezzlement, there is no system which will stop a foolish cashier from putting his hand in the till. Our cashier had been in his post for five years and was well aware that he was subject to surprise inspections once a month. That system ensured 1) that any deficiency would be discovered within a month at longest, 2) that the amount taken would be kept small and 3) that the chances of recovery would be greatly enhanced. No administration can do more. No fault could be placed on our administration and not a penny of public funds was lost.

All these apparent irregularities got headlines in the media, clearly from information supplied by a disgruntled insider, leaving a cumulative impression of total incompetence. Their complete rebuttal, if reported at all, received only a couple of lines, and usually not in a prominent position. Thus the Minister was correct in saying that a cloud was left over the staff. It was obvious that however tenuous and flimsy the 'evidence' for the alleged fraud the Government had no option but to bring it to court, otherwise Lindsay would have accused the Gobernment of concealing evidence unfavourable to them. But the media gave no worthwhile publicity to the rebuttal of the charges and the public were left to believe them.

It was a year and a half of seemingly endless strain. I had begun to wonder whether the campaign would ever end. As the allegations were being made by a former Minister, who was also a Senior Counsel, the public naturally thought 'There must be something in it.' I told that Conor Cruise O'Brien had said 'that poor man Harry Boylan is having a terrible time,' Two years later he was having his own turn and resigned from the Department of External Affairs in order to be free to defend himself publicly against criticism of his actions as UN Representative in Katanga, Congo.

The worst feature for me was my feeling of total helplessness. I could do nothing except wait for the next blow. I was acutely aware that as Director I was personally accountable to the Minister for the conduct and management of Gaeltarra business. My career was on the line from the beginning to the end of the Lindsay campaign. Our children, aged nine to nineteen, could read the newspapers. Children are quick to notice that their parents are worried. Hugo, the eldest, still recalls my going to the phone to receive a call from Donegal and my return to the dining-room with my face 'white as a sheet'. It was, of course, the message of Fricker's suicide. Patricia's unswerving support made home a haven of calm, good cheer and reassurance. I did not quite realise how she had been affected until it was all over and I had moved to Finance when she said vehemently, 'I don't want to hear the name of that place mentioned ever again.'

In 1959, after a short period in the Department of the Gaeltacht, I was seconded to a Department of Finance task force. In 1958, T. K. Whitaker, Secretary of the Department of Finance and head of the Civil Service, had published, with Government consent, a survey entitled *Economic Development*. Based on this report the Government approved and published its first *Programme for Economic Development*, which was received with wide public approval. Whitaker, aware of the danger that like so many Government reports, this programme might be put on a shelf and allowed to gather dust, set up a small task force to oversee its implementation.

It was headed by C. H. Murray, who later became Secretary of the Department of Finance and Governor of the Central Bank. The staff included Maurice Doyle, who, in due course, succeeded to the same appointments, Dr Louden Ryan, on secondment from TCD, where he was Professor of Economics, and Luke Leonard, later a senior economist with the World Bank in Washington. I brought to this élite, high-powered group direct experience of industrial production, relations with staff and trade unions and their importance, and successful promotion of exports. The work, as might be expected in that company, was very demanding, but stimulating and very various—I remember working very hard on a paper on industrial training which was well received—and I enjoyed my two years there and profited from the experience. I then returned to the Department of Lands as Principal Officer in the Land Commission in 1961 and all this time retained my directorship in Arramara, which continued to flourish. Promotion to Assistant Secretary followed not too long afterwards, with involvement in the new concept of conservation in all its aspects.

Picture Section

My father, Captain John Boylan (bareheaded, seated third from right), and his crew on board the Dun Cow, *a three-masted tea-clipper. The photograph was taken in San Francisco in the 1890s. At this time, officers and crew did not wear uniform, but my father's position in the photograph shows that he is Captain. The crew always referred to the Captain as 'the Old Man' be he twenty-five or fifty.*

The family tombstone in Mornington graveyard. The inscription reads:
Erected by Capt. Peter Boylan of Baltray in memory of his Father, Capt. William
Boylan who departed this life the 5th of August 1832 aged 30 years. Also to the
memory of his Niece Kate Boylan who died January 18th 1860 aged 4 months.
And also to the memory of his Sister Catherine Freeman who departed this life the
25th of March 1861 aged 28 years. William Joseph Boylan died 1st July 1869
aged 7 years and 10 Months. Capt. William Boylan [my grandfather] *Brother of*
the above named Peter, died Jan 16 1889. Also Capt. John Boylan [my father]
who died 23 Oct. 1945 aged 81 years Mary Catherine Boylan [my sister May]
daughter of the above who died 1 March 1982 and her brother John Francis
Boylan [my brother Jack] *who died 14 May 1984 aged 75 years.* (Photograph:
Kato Boylan)

My parents on their wedding day in 1900.

Riverside: our home in Drogheda. This photograph was taken in the mid-1990s. When we were growing up there was an open grass-covered park of about three or four acres across the road in front of the house. It stretched from the Viaduct to a high wall behind which were coal yards. A narrow road leading under the Viaduct into Donors Green separated this grassy space from the Ballast Quay and the river. We played cricket on it on summer days. (Photograph: Hugo Boylan)

'The Old Man': my father in Captain's uniform, aged about sixty.

Dancing on the pier at Clogher Head in the 1930s. (Photograph: Maurice Curtin)

Picture No. 34   Regatta day from the competitor's viewpoint as they prepared for the race

Regatta day on the Boyne. (Photograph: Des Clinton)

The silver medal I won at the Dublin University Boat Club Regatta, 1933.

The gold medal I won at the Tailteann Games 1932.

The caption to this press cutting from June 1933 reads: JUNIOR SCULLING CHAMPION *H. Boylan (Dublin Rowing Club) snapped after passing the post to win the Phoenix Challenge Cup at the D.U.B.C.* (Photograph: Irish Independent)

Left: Willy in his Captain's uniform, with medal ribbons.

Below: Willy was Captain of the Yorktown *when she was torpedoed in the Atlantic in 1942. The crew took to lifeboats and rafts. Here Willy is pictured (2nd from left) with a fellow crew member (looking at Willy) and the bomber aircrew who spotted their liferaft in the sea and relayed its position to the destroyer which rescued them.*

Going away photograph, after our wedding on 18 September 1941.
Front, left to right: my parents, myself and Patricia and my sister Una; behind Patricia is her mother and her brother Phaudes.
Next row: Mollie Clancy; Clare and Basil Clancy (themselves recently married); just behind Basil is Eithne Keane, daughter of my sister Kitty; beside her is Patricia's father (with bow tie) and beside him is Patricia's brother Kevin.
Next row: Nan Boylan, Joe Boylan; Kitty Keane; May Boylan; Pauline Cullen (half hidden) Nina Clancy. Behind Joe is the Curate, next to him is Kitty Boylan (Tom's wife).
Back row; Fr Paddy Murray; Jack Keane; Tom Boylan; Joe Clancy; Jack Clancy.

The Phantom of the Opera! Conferring of MA, Trinity College Dublin, 1948.

January 1942: The Dublin Verse Speaking Society commemorates the death of W. B. Yeats (from left) Patricia, Robert Mooney, Austin Clarke, Eithne Dunne, Ruaidhri Roberts, Laurence Elyan and Florence Lynch. (Photograph: The Irish Times)

Director of Gaeltacht Services 1952. On my desk is a sketch showing a dress made from Donegal tweed. (Photograph: Irish Press)

At Shannon Airport 1956. Left to right: myself, Liam Morrissey, Coras Tráchtála, Robert Briscoe TD, Lord Mayor of Dublin, Major Kirkwood, T. J. O'Driscoll, Director General of Bord Fáilte.

The children in 1951. Left to right: Hugo, Anna, Peter, Kato. (Photograph: Lorna Madden)

After an Annual General Meeting of Arramara. Left to right: Alan Stewart, Minister Tom O'Donnell TD, Ralph Merton, Charlie Cameron, myself. (Photograph: Lensman)

An academic escort: Professor Tomás de Bhaldraithe, myself and Professor Kevin B. Nowlan.

Early 1980s: leaving Dún Laoghaire harbour in the Ruffian with my eldest grandson, Jonathan, at the helm.

Patricia and I at the Merriman Summer School 2001. (Photograph John Horgan)

8 Wild Life and Game Birds

My last assignment in the Civil Service was to oversee the country's first tentative steps into the environment field. Although many Irish people knew and loved their local wildlife, there was a tendency to regard nature conservation as the preserve of the hunting and shooting set. As the Minister put it at a conference we organised 'until a few years ago wildlife, in so far as anybody gave it any thought, was something that God put there and that, like the grass, "just growed". In Ireland, at any rate, there was little pressure brought to bear on it other than by a handful of sportsmen and so wild animals and birds were largely able to pursue their own separate lives with little interference from humankind.' Of course as the effects of the Whitaker economic reforms filtered across the country, development began to put different pressures on the natural world.

But there was still a strong connection with the fishing and shooting lobbies. Shortly before I became Assistant Secretary, Ireland had become affiliated to the Conseil International de la Chasse et de La Nature, occasioned by a new recognition of the importance of conservation of our inheritance of abundant wild life and large areas of significance to scientists and ecologists (and of course tourists). At the time An Taisce (the National Trust for Ireland) and Foras Forbartha (the National Institute for Physical Planning and Construction Research) were the only organisations with any interest in the physical environment. The wits in the Land Commission said that this meant looking after Wild Life and Game Birds and no better man for this than Boylan. With me were Fergus O'Gorman as Scientific Officer and Con Connolly, Assistant Principal.

The process of finding out what other countries were doing entailed at least two enjoyable trips abroad. The General Assembly of the Conseil for 1969 was held in Paris and suitable entertainment was provided for delegates (some of whom attended in full hunting dress), including a cocktail party at the residence of the Baron and Baroness de Rothschild and a banquet at the Maison de La Chasse. The following year the Conseil held a Conference in Budapest, capital of the People's Republic of Hungary. Fergus and Con and I stayed in a hotel on the banks of the Danube and from my window I saw racing eights training in the evening, recalling for me my rowing days of the Thirties. We were assigned a guide from the National Tourist Office, a very courteous, gentle, elderly man, who clearly had seen better days. He took a group of us on a conducted tour of Buda, the old part of the city, a historical town of palaces, churches, museums and parks. He had good English, as well as German and French and spoke of Buda with knowledge and affection. Later, I discovered that he was or had been the Margrave of Altmark, Margrave being the hereditary title of certain princes of the Holy Roman Empire. There was no place for such a figure from the past in Communist dominated Hungary. His knowledge of languages was probably his sole passport to employment.

I arranged a small drinks party on behalf of the Irish delegation and invited him to it. Ten minutes before the party, Con Connolly, our linguist with fluent French and German, phoned from his room in a weak whisper to say that he had lost his voice and couldn't come. I urged him to come, if only for a half-hour, saying that a few glasses of Hungarian wine would do him good. At first he demurred but after further persuasion agreed to put in an appearance. He was standing beside me when the Margrave arrived with his Margravine. The Margrave wore his dress uniform with its gold facings, and decorations. His wife was a vision from a vanished Hungarian nobility. She was tall, slender, elegant in a white evening dress and long white gloves. She must have been a beautiful woman before the ravages of misfortune took their toll, and she was still a striking figure. I presented Con to her. He bowed and clicked his heels. She smiled and extended her hand to him, palm down. He kissed it and to my astonishment his voice instantly came back and he welcomed the Margravine in a torrent of fluent German. I said to myself 'This must be the greatest miracle since Moses struck the rock in the desert and water gushed forth.' I left all three of them in the animated conversation of re-united old friends.

In 1968, I was elected Chairman of the Commissioners of the Wexford North Slob, an area of 2,470 acres of muddy flats reclaimed from the sea in the 1840s. How did this come about? The year before, William Finlay SC and Major Robin Ruttledge, of the Irish Wildbird Conservancy, had approached the Department of Lands to convey their concern at the continuing decrease in the number of Greenland white-fronted geese wintering on the North Slob. Europe's rarest goose, one third of the world population of these 'magnificent, shy and family-oriented birds' had been spending from October to the following April on the North Slob. The Conservancy sought the assistance of the Department in countering this unwelcome fall in their numbers as well as help in restoring the sea wall to good condition. Our response was immediate and positive. The Land Commission was of course well used to buying land, and so acquired 270 acres of the Slob in 1968 and later another 200. In 1969, in association with the Conservancy, we began the setting up of the Wexford Wildfowl Reserve.

The Slob is administered by a Commission established under the Wexford Embankment Act of 1852. This was the culmination of nearly fifty years of trying to reclaim the areas just north and south of Wexford harbour (paradoxically, the success of the reclamation was a key cause of the silting up of Wexford harbour).

Every owner of fifty acres or more on the Slob is entitled to be a Commissioner and I was nominated as the Department's representative. The Commission's main function is to maintain the sea wall, the internal roads, the pumping station, sluice gates and fresh water canal of this miniature Zuider Zee. It levies a rate on the land owners to finance this work.

I attended my first meeting of the Commission early in 1968 and received a warm welcome from the friendly members. After I had been given a conducted tour of the Slob, the formal business began and the others unanimously insisted on electing me Chairman as representing the Department, the largest landowner. On return to Dublin, I duly reported to the Minister and Secretary of the Department my election as Chairman and they nodded their heads in grave approval. I added a feeble joke. 'I think I am now entitled to call myself the Chief Slob.' This touch of levity on a matter of important State business went down like the proverbial lead balloon. My welcome at home, with half-a-dozen unplucked widgeon from the Slobs, to be prepared and cooked, was not much warmer.

After my retirement from the Civil Service in 1972, I lost official contact with the Slob Commission but read with interest the occasional press report of the progress of the Wildfowl Reserve and resolved to make another trip to Wexford. But time passed and good resolutions remained unfulfilled until early in October 2000, I made the return trip to Wexford, accompanied by Kato and her friend Mary Oduka from Uganda. We were shown round by Tim Collins, exchange Warden from Australia. On my previous visit thirty-two years previously, facilities for visitors were virtually non-existent. Now there is a fine visitors' centre with exhibits of great interest, including a punt gun twelve feet long, a fearsome weapon now banned. I learned that the Wildfowl Reserve was officially opened in 1974, that careful management had brought the wintering Greenland white-fronts to a total of 10,000 from a low of 6,000 in the 1979s, that the Reserve now extends to 470 acres and its international fame attracts 24,000 visitors annually.

Several hundred white-fronts had already arrived and Tim told us that they had made an unbroken flight of 2,000 miles in 17 hours. Birds return to the same field as in previous years and to the same corner of that field. They will not graze in long grass as with heads down they cannot see round them and this restricted vision would leave them vulnerable. The Warden arranges to have cows graze the pasture before the Greenland geese and others arrive.

The Slob, low-lying with sandbars and mud flats, is very attractive to wild fowl and thousands of ducks, geese, swans and waders winter there, attracted also by the prevailing mild winters. One can spend hours simply watching the great flocks of wintering birds swooping down from the sky to this wide tract of land reserved for their protection. And it was no small pleasure to look back to my initial involvement and to appreciate how capably that foundation had been built upon by the State and dedicated voluntary organisations, Bird Watch Ireland, and the Irish Wild Life Trust. William Finlay is still associated with them, and Major Robin Ruttledge died recently in his 103rd year. When the Royal Society for the Protection of Birds opened an office in Monkstown, Co. Dublin some years ago, they named it Ruttledge House.

In 1970 the Department organised a big conference of international and local experts to explore the way we should develop our conservation policy. The assembled 'great and good' were from all over—TCD, UCD, Belfast, Edinburgh, Oxford, London, Washington, Wisconsin. Before the conference we took them in coaches around all the sites of special interest—raised bog, the Burren, natural forests, eskers and so on; then we ended up in the Great Southern in Killarney for three days. The Minister set the agenda in his opening speech in terms which make it clear how new all this was to Ireland: 'non-shooting people in Ireland are beginning to take an interest in this other strange and beautiful life beyond their doorsteps. Above all, Ireland, launched lately on a programme of industrial and commercial expansion, is finding that uncontrolled development of factories and power plants, tourist resorts, drainage schemes and industrialised farming, can spell death to this other life as readily in Ireland as elsewhere.' At the end of the conference a series of recommendations was drawn up, and much of the subsequent organisational development stemmed from that.

Although it is now thirty years since my official connection with conservation policy, I felt disappointed at reading in *The Irish Times* (3 December 2001) that the European Commission had formally reprimanded the Republic for failing to protect the country's wild bird population and for not adopting and implementing a crucial national heritage plan.

During the conference I became very friendly with the Chairman, the world-famous naturalist F. Fraser Darling, who was at that time with the Conservation Foundation in Washington. He came to dinner with us in Dublin and afterwards gave me an inscribed copy of *The Hobbit* by J. R. R. Tolkien—he raved about the book, but this was not an author I could get on with at all.

Interlude: Oh! No Minister

This was published in *Dublin Opinion* in June 1987.

John Benignus Rooney walked purposefully up Merrion Street to his office in the great Department of Ways and Means. He thought with pleasure of the morning's work ahead. Five Parliamentary Questions to be answered! He, JB Rooney, was the acknowledged master of the genre; his rule—"the minimum of information with the maximum of wordage". The Times *crossword was rewarding; drafting answers to PQs was a feast. He had begun to think lately of publishing a monograph on the art, in retirement of course. A slim volume—Rooney on PQs. He could see it prescribed for courses in Colleges of Administration.*

Yes, Rooney on the PQ, *like* Blackstone on the Laws of England.

Arrived at the office, he laid out the tools of his craft; six sheets of ruled foolscap, his Shaeffer fountain pen, the Standing Orders for Dáil Procedure and Chambers' Dictionary.

The phrases flowed smoothly:

"If the Deputy will kindly advert to my reply to his previous question of the sixteenth ultimo—"

"The policy of my Department in regard to this virtually intractable problem was adumbrated—"

Adumbrated—that will poleaxe them!

"Was adumbrated in my address last week to the Amalgamated Society of Window Dressers."

"I deprecate the tone of the representations addressed to me on this matter . . . "

As a beginner, he had tried garnishing and enriching his drafts with

Latin and French tags:

Mutatis mutandis, faute de mieux, etc.

But his then chief, a low fellow from Carlow, had reacted violently. Now he used English only, which to his ear sounded great organ notes in his rounded sentences. By one o'clock he had finished and magisterial drafts were dispatched to the Minister's office.

After lunch, as he walked back across St Stephen's Green, two senior Revenue Commissioners passed by, casting suspicious looks at the ducks on the pond. From a side path there emerged the Governor of the Central Bank, deep in conversation with the Governor of the Bank of Ireland. This was a rich day.

He had hardly sat down at his desk when the telephone rang. His junior answered and turned pale. He put his hand over the mouthpiece and whispered:

"It's the Minister. For you."

JB was not easily alarmed after twenty years of dicing with death in these corridors of power, but yet his finely chiselled features twitched as he took the telephone.

"Yes, Minister?"

"Mother o'God, Rooney, I've just got a load of stuff that no Christian could understand."

The accent was unmistakable. The new Minister!

"What parts do you find difficult, Minister?"

"The whole flaming lot, Rooney, the whole flaming lot. I'll give out my own answers, in my own words."

"Oh, no! Minister."

But the phone went dead. Why did he ring him *and not the Head of the whole Department, the Rúnaí? Of course, a Gaeilgoir, he had asked for Rúnaí and got Rooney. What would this savage from the South do with his carefully constructed phrases? What bog-English would he bellow across the floor of the House? The telephone rang again. This time it was the real Rúnaí. His voice was tense.*

"Rooney. The Minister," he swallowed. "The Minister is going to

answer those questions with just 'Yes' or 'No'."

"My God," gasped JB. "Could he not be talked into saying, at least: 'The answer is in the affirmative'?"

"No, I reasoned with him, but his language just got worse. Listen to the radio at six for the Dáil report."

His voice trailed off. He seemed on the verge of breaking down.

JB stared at his dictionary, his Standing Orders. His life's work lay in ruins. Farewell to visions of modest fame. A miasma of monosyllables shimmered before him. What was left to him now? He was far too old to run away to sea. Should he end the whole sorry farce in the only way open to a man of honour?

At last it was almost six o'clock. He tottered to the coffee room to listen to the Dáil report. He heard the questions called and the mountainy voice:

"YES . . . NO . . . YES . . . YES . . . NO."

"Oh, no! Minister," he moaned.

At midnight, JB found himself lying on the pavement outside a public house. He did not know how he had got there. An enormous Garda loomed over him.

"Would you like me to get a taxi for you, sir?"

JB struggled to his feet. Gathering his strength he said with dignity:

"The answer is in the affirmative, the affirmative, the affirmative."

That is what he always says when visitors address him in the large house where he lives now:

"The answer is in the affirmative, the affirmative, the affirmative."

When he breaks down and cries heartrendingly:

"Oh, no! Minister."

The attendants smile understandingly and lead him gently back to his room.

9 A New Career

I retired from the Civil Service in April 1972, at the age of sixty, then the earliest age at which one could retire without losing pension rights. I continued for ten years as Director of Arramara but it remained a part-time post and I began to write. I relished the freedom to go my own way, the release from the daily office round, although I was fortunate that my appointments had brought much travel and acquaintance with people from worlds far removed from the ordered pace of life in a long-established Government Department. In Radio Éireann it was everyday contact with writers, poets, musicians. Arramara and Gaeltarra introduced me to the world of business, sharpened my wits and brought me enduring friendships.

Just before I retired Gill & Macmillan had conceived the idea of publishing a *Dictionary of Irish Biography*, as none had appeared since Dr John Crone's *Concise Dictionary of Irish Biography* of 1928, itself a successor to Alfred John Webb's *Compendium of Irish Biography* of 1878. My daughter Anna was then a Managing Editor in Gill & Macmillan and asked me if I would be interested in compiling the Dictionary. I thought about it, and, little knowing how much work it would turn out to be, said I would, conscious that I would have plenty of leisure quite soon. In January 1972 Anna married Tony Farmar and left for Nigeria, so when I signed a contract with G&M I was assigned to Mary Dowey as my editor. I soon found that the Dictionary was a major undertaking, requiring many hours of research; I found myself spending almost all my days in Trinity and the National Library. Eventually I looked around for an assistant. I was fortunate to get the services of Margaret Coffey, a young

Australian on a studentship in Dublin.

My first big problem was to decide who to include. As a definition of Irishness, Conor Cruise O'Brien had recently proposed the concept: 'Irishness is not primarily a question of birth or blood or language: it is the condition of being involved in the Irish situation and usually of being mauled by it.' This picturesque but unsafe criterion would include a long list of English from Elizabeth's Earl of Essex to Augustine Birrell. So I stuck to a broad criterion of being born in Ireland or possession of an Irish parent. I finally decided on birth in Ireland, or of Irish descent, or Irish parent, and those who lived and worked in Ireland or made a considerable contribution to Irish life. In the Preface I list the many friends who helped and encouraged, lending books and indicating useful sources. Some had fun pulling my leg like Tomás de Bhaldraithe who gave me an enthusiastic description of a great man from the Glen of Aherlow who had six All-Ireland medals and could dance a step dance and sing in great voice at the age of 100. He, said Tomás, should *definitely* be included. Tomás's serious comments were among the most valued. When the research had been done and all the information, dates and achievements assembled, there remained the writing of the entry. The writing of each entry demanded scrupulous care, accuracy, a feeling for the person being put before the world and an overwhelming compulsion to present a truthful picture and ensure that justice is done.

After six years work, the first edition appeared in 1978 and to my great relief was, on the whole, warmly welcomed. Oddly it was described as 'edited by Henry Boylan', though I had written every word myself. Eileen Battersby queried me on this point when interviewing me for *The Irish Times* when the third edition was published in 1998 and in her article said, 'Surely the book widely known as "Boylan's Dictionary of Irish Biography" should be entitled exactly that.' The point had not struck me until Eileen pointed it out.

One review that particularly pleased me was by William Trevor in *The Oldie*. He described the *Dictionary* as 'splendid' and remarked:

> Such reference books tend to be staid—solemn gatherings of business chiefs and grey politicians, the Establishment reverentially dragged out of its severely reserved bone-orchard. Everyone in Mr Boylan's particular graveyard is dead too, but his obituarist's style is so lively you'd hardly know it.

Also in 1978, I took part in a lecture tour organised by a group of Irish-Americans in Boston. We spoke at a number of schools and colleges in Massachusetts and New York State, and ended up at a week-long conference in London, Ontario where I found myself in the company of such Irish notables as John McGahern and Professor Kevin B. Nowlan, along with a number of well-known US and Canadian academics. American sales benefited from this safari and at the end I felt that I was really launched on a new career as a writer.

Shortly after the publication of the Dictionary, Gill & Macmillan invited me to contribute a biography of Theobald Wolfe Tone to their new Irish Lives series. This was published in 1981. I may say that from the Dictionary on, I never had any difficulty in finding a publisher. Some time later, we were at a lunch in the United Arts Club at which Séamus Heaney read a number of new, unpublished poems. One was entitled 'Wolfe Tone' and after reading it, Séamus handed me his typescript, having signed it with a pleasing dedication to Patricia and myself and a note of admiration for my book. The poem appeared in his collection *The Haw Lantern* (1987). I told him that in the days of sail when a ship was nearing port after a voyage of twelve months or more an old salt was sure to say in the fo'c's'le 'when I get ashore I'm going to buy an oar, put it on my shoulder, and set out to the country. When I'm stopped by a man who asks me "What's that quare yoke there on your shoulder", I'll settle in that place and never go to sea again.' Séamus told me that 'the shouldered oar' (line 7 in his poem) appears in Homer's *Odyssey* when Ulysses returns to Ithaca after twenty years at sea and was fascinated to hear that this concept from the classics had come down among seafarers until the 1880s.

Wolfe Tone

for Harry and Pat with love—and admiration for WT (the book).

Séamus 10 January 1987 in United Arts Club.

Light as a skiff, manoeuvrable
yet outmanoeuvred,

I affected epaulettes and a cockade,
wrote a style well-bred and impervious

to the solidarity I angled for
and played the ancient Roman with a razor.

I was the shouldered oar that ended up
far from the brine and whiff of venture,

like a scratching post or a crossroads flagpole,
out of my element among small farmers—

I who wakened once to the shouts of men
rising from the bottom of the sea,

men in their shirts mounting through deep water
when the Atlantic stove our cabin's dead lights in

and the big fleet split and Ireland dwindled
as we ran before the gale under bare poles.

When the Rising of 1798 was being commemorated, I suggested to Gill & Macmillan that it would be a suitable opportunity to issue a reprint. They agreed and I asked Séamus for permission to include his poem as a preface, a permission he gave at once.

I was quite astonished when in 1993 the Royal National Institute for the Blind applied for permission to produce Braille and Moon transcriptions of this biography of the man who has been described as 'the father of Irish Republicanism' and 'the Prophet of Irish Independence'. In accordance with practice, permission was given free of charge or royalty. I hope that the clients of the Institute benefited from reading this Life and that it gave them a a better understanding of 'the Irish Question'. And I was quite impressed that the Institute should be concerned to put such a book with its ringing call, 'to break the connection with England, the never-failing source of all our political evils', into the hands of their English readers.

Nineteen-eighty-seven saw an attempt to revive *Dublin Opinion*, a well-loved and successful humorous monthly, edited by Tom Collins and Charlie Kelly from 1926 until 1968, when it was voluntarily wound up by them. They were then both over normal retirement age. Collins contributed poems, stories and articles and set the tone, gentle humour rather than satire. Kelly's cartoons reflected this approach, but from time to time had a sharper edge in commenting on current events. I contributed to the first issue of the revived *Dublin Opinion* which appeared in May 1987 and to further numbers that year. Early in 1988 I was invited to an editorial conference in The Grey Door, a smart restaurant in Pembroke Street. It took place in a private room, which seemed a very good beginning and the party included, as well as the editor, Bob Ryan, Frank Kelly, son of Charlie Kelly of the original *Opinion* and a contributor like myself, another contributor, several secretaries and a man I took to be the 'money-man'. Drinks appeared, followed by a very good lunch and well-chosen wine. The conversation was lively, the company in high good humour and why not, with such a reception. I thought of the famous *Punch* luncheons, so renowned for their sparkling talk that household names intrigued to secure invitations.

I was basking in thoughts of being part of such an agreeable development in Dublin when the company was, as it were, called to order by my money-man, who had spoken little during the lunch and now took charge. He told us, not wasting any words, that the new *Dublin Opinion* had been losing money steadily since its revival, that advertisements were falling off with weakening sales and that he could not afford to continue his support unless there was an immediate and distinct improvement. This came as a complete shock and surprise to me, and I think to the other contributors present. In plain words, we were attending, not a conference on future issues, but a rehearsal of a wake. My fond vision of a series of *Punch*-like luncheons vanished instantly. Our man proceeded bluntly to say that he would support, at most, only two or three further issues and we took our departure, deflated. The magazine finally folded after three more issues at long intervals. Looking back, I think that the revival failed simply because there is no longer a readership like that which enjoyed and supported the original. We seem now to be vastly more sophisticated, knowledgeable and cynical. *Punch*, has gone, probably for much the same reasons. Neither has been replaced, their day is gone.

My next publication was *This Arrogant City, a Readers' and Collectors' Guide to Books about Dublin* which was published by Anna and Tony. I took the title from 'Dublin Made Me', a poem by Donagh MacDonagh (The *Oxford Book of Irish Verse*, 1958), 'the Dublin of old statutes, this arrogant city, stirs proudly and secretly in my blood.' The Introduction begins, 'Many people have been inspired or infuriated by Dublin to the extent of writing a book about it', and I selected fifty titles by a wide variety of writers, native Dubliners, exiles from Dublin, some who left and came back, others who departed for good, but carried the city with them, the most famous being, of course, James Joyce, and visitors from England, China and the USA. *This Arrogant City*, includes prints of buildings, street architecture, of a group of small children playing Ring-a-Ring-of-Roses in the street and a reproduction of a grim little invitation card to a funeral, adorned with skeletons, urns, Father Time, mourning coaches and weeping cherubs. My part in the production was limited to selecting the books and authors and writing a brief introductory note to each. A strongly bound paper back at four by eight inches, it was designed to fit snugly into the pocket, and all-in-all I thought it was, and still is, a very attractive book.

Having been born in Drogheda and spent my teenage years rowing and fishing on the Boyne and exploring its upper reaches, I read with special interest Sir William Wilde's *The Beauties of the Boyne and its tributary, the Blackwater*, published in 1849. I suggested to Michael O'Brien of O'Brien Press that the time was ripe for a new, up-to-date and comprehensive study of the Boyne Valley and its five thousand years of history. Michael agreed and I set about the undertaking.

I was rather taken with Sir William's suggestion that a Dublin resident could visit all the places of interest in the Boyne Valley comfortably in three days, travelling by railway and then hiring an outside jaunting car. I had no doubt but that to see the Valley of the Boyne and savour its astonishing wealth of history one should traverse the course of the river from source to sea. But I parted company with Sir William as to the time to take. It seemed very strange to me that in 1849, a time which we tend to look back on as one when people were free from our daily frantic pace, he counselled what can only be described as a headlong, hurried rush to see as much as possible in three days. His plan included everything from the source of the Boyne, to Moyvalley, Trim, Navan, Tara, Newgrange, Knowth, the field of the Battle of the Boyne, Mellifont and back to Drogheda in time to catch the last train to Dublin—all, so he claimed, to be done in three days! My own progress was leisurely, with digressions and turnings aside, as recollections of 'old, unhappy, far-off things and battles long ago', crowded in the memory.

A Valley of Kings, The Boyne, was published in 1988 and was favourably received. As might be expected, many of the illustrations came from the invaluable Laurence Collection. Particularly pleasing is a photograph of a beautiful old bridge across the Boyne canal, only a few minutes walk from the main road outside Navan. Despite being so close to the main road, it can be easily missed. And a photograph by Maurice Curtin of couples dancing on Clogher Head pier on a summer evening in the Thirties evokes unsophisticated pleasures that seem to belong to a faraway past. Also included are engravings from Wilde's book, the work of artist and antiquary William Wakeman which, while they may not have the detail and accuracy of modern archaeological work, capture, with great sympathy, the beauty and mystery of the places depicted. At the launch of the late Breandán Ó hEithir's second novel *Sionnach ar mo Dhuán* that same year of 1988, he inscribed my copy '*Don fhear a bhuaigh Cath na Bóinne i 1988*' ('To the man who won the Battle of the Boyne in 1988').

My next book arose out of my long membership of the Royal Irish Yacht Club. We had left our large house in Orwell Park in 1979 and moved to York Road, Dún Laoghaire, seven miles from the centre of town. It took a bit of getting used to the smaller rooms in this warm and comfortable house after the Victorian splendours of Orwell Park, but with children gone and the heating and endless maintenance becoming more troublesome, a move seemed a good idea. So we arrived much nearer to boats and the sea, which have been a recurring theme in this memoir. We now made greater use of the Club. I had for years been a keen member of the Mermaid fleet, having first sailed in this 17 ft half-decked sloop class with the Trinity Sailing Club. I joined the Dublin Bay Sailing Club in 1964 and the Royal Irish in 1969. Sailing became my major pastime. My fellow-owner, Bob Curran of the Department of Finance, and I raced on

Thursdays and Saturdays throughout the season, and I took my turn as Class Captain in 1976. As I got on a bit I thought I would move over to the larger, more modern Ruffian class, so I bought one in Cork which I raced for a few seasons, but found it harder and harder to get crew, so as I reached my seventieth year I hung up my oilskins for the last time, after nearly thirty enjoyable years in 'the Bay'.

Early in 1989, the Club Commodore, Robert Barr, asked me on behalf of the Committee, to undertake a history of the Club. My only question was whether the Club records were well kept, and when he assured me that they were I was delighted to accept the commission. The Committee set up a History Sub-Committee of three, Mr Justice Barr, Fergus McKinley and Clive Martin. I found the history of the Club fascinating, as revealed in the records, and from other sources and the knowledge of the History Sub-Committee, all former flag officers. They supplied Club folklore not to be found in formal records and all the more entertaining on that account. Finding a title bothered me for quite a while. Obviously, '*A History of the Royal Irish Yacht Club*' had to be included, but by itself I thought it might be off-putting, perhaps suggesting a formal, academic approach. Eventually I settled on a quotation from a poem by Robert Bridges, 'A Passer By',

> '*Whither, O splendid ship, thy white sails crowding,*
> *Leaning across the bosom of the urgent West,*
> *That fearest nor sea rising, nor sky clouding,*
> *Whither away, fair rover, and what thy quest?*'

On the jacket, the title, *White Sails Crowding, A History of the Royal Irish Yacht Club* appears under a picture of the leading yachts rounding the flagship in the Club Regatta of 1873, and these 'White Sails Crowding', were familiar to me as the picture, a large oil painting by Richard Brydges Beechey, hangs in the Club drawing room, and I had studied it with interest many times.

The Club was founded in 1831 but its activities ceased in 1840 and it remained dormant until 1846 when it was revived by a group of prominent merchants and professional men, including the Liberator Daniel O'Connell, two of his sons and a number of Quakers. Queen Victoria and Prince Albert agreed to become Joint Patrons and the Marquess of Donegal became Commodore. The resurgence of the Club came about because a number of rising men became dissatisfied with their exclusion from certain circles and clubs on the grounds that they did not come from the landed gentry or were not part of the Establishment as symbolised by Dublin Castle. Like the great Edmund Burke (1729–97) they were 'new men', relying for advancement on their own ability and industry and not on inherited position or wealth, but nonetheless standing for traditional values and opposed to revolution.

But it also included men of strong Nationalist sympathies, such as Canon James A. Hannay (1865–1950), an active member of the Gaelic League from its foundation in 1893 by Douglas Hyde, a close friend of his from their undergraduate days at TCD. He sailed a Water Wag in Dublin Bay and became famous as a novelist under the pen name George H. Birmingham.

A notable member was Sir Thomas Lipton, elected in 1906. He was born in a tenement in Glasgow, son of a poor Irish labourer. Starting with a small grocer's shop, his hard work, long hours, and business acumen made him a millionaire by the age of thirty. In his late forties he developed an all-absorbing interest in yachting and made five unsuccessful challenges for the America's Cup in his famous 'Shamrock' yachts. He became immensely popular in America for his sporting spirit and at home won wide recognition for his liberal philanthropy, being created a knight in 1898 and a baronet in 1902. He was finally elected by acclamation to the Royal Yacht Squadron at the age of eighty having been rejected for many years. This was generally regarded as a tardy recognition of a great sportsman. The Royal Irish had no difficulty in electing him in 1906 and he remained a member until his death in 1934.

Members of the Club served in British forces during the First World War, but before its outbreak several became gun-runners for the Irish Volunteers. In July and August 1914 three yachts, the *Asgard*, the *Kelpie* and the *Chotah* took part in the landing of guns and ammunition on the east coast. The *Asgard*, sailed by Erskine Childers, and the *Kelpie* under Conor O'Brien between them collected a cargo of munitions from a German tug off the Belgian coast. The *Asgard* landed her share at Howth on 21 July 1914 and the *Kelpie* transhipped her share to the *Chotah*, sailed by Sir Thomas Myles, FRCSI. He landed it at Kilcoole, Co. Wicklow, where it was received by a company of Volunteers under Seán T. O'Kelly, later second President of the Irish Republic. Sir Thomas was knighted in 1902, was Hon. Surgeon in Ireland to King George V and a member of the Club from 1905. He was assisted by James Creed Meredith KC, later a judge of the Supreme Court, who joined the Club in 1932. Conor O'Brien joined in 1923 and won fame for his cruise around the world, 1923–5. He was a grandson of William Smith O'Brien, the Young Irelander, and an original member of Sinn Féin. Erskine Childers was the author of *The Riddle of the Sands*. His son Erskine became fourth President of Ireland.

Erskine Childers and Conor O'Brien joined the Royal Navy shortly after these exploits and served with distinction for the whole of the First World War. Their fellow naval officers, including, no doubt, members of the Royal Irish, would have been quite baffled by their gun-running activities.

The historian, F. S. L. Lyons, posed the question, 'Why was this strange episode, on which it can be said without exaggeration, turned the whole future of the Irish insurrection, so largely in the hands of the Irish ascendency class?' He saw it as

> a reaction to the equally illegal landing of arms in April 1914 for the Ulster Volunteer Force, using the threat of force with absolute immunity and complete success. Employed in the South it might help to stiffen the determination of Asquith and his colleagues in following out their policy of Home Rule. And, of course, if shipping arms illegally to Ireland added a spice of excitement to comfortable aristocratic lives, so much the better. But that the arms might actually go off in other hands than theirs, seems not to have entered their calculations.

White Sails Crowding appeared in 1994 and has had a steady sale, new members being the most regular purchasers.

In between these major commitments, I continued steady research for the next edition of the Dictionary, having perhaps a macabre interest in reports on the deaths of possible candidates for inclusion in the next edition. Editions were published in 1988 and in 1998, the latter with the welcome addition of illustrations. The entries had increased from about 1,100 in the first to over 1,700 in the third edition.

Interlude: Bed & Board

First published in *Dublin Opinion* July/August 1987

It all began at a party when I was introduced to Laetitia. Tall, lean, almost raw-boned, she instantly put me in mind of a woman explorer. So I was quite astonished when she said immediately:

'I must sit down. Parties I like, but all this standing. It's my back.'

It seemed that she had to sleep on a board. To keep her spine straight.

I confided that I'd had a sharp attack of sciatica myself a fortnight before. Had to crawl upstairs on my hands and knees. Two days in bed with an electric blanket. No, I was fine now. First time it ever happened to me.

Laetitia looked at me with flattering concern.

'I'd take care if I were you. It could strike again.'

'You'd recommend a board for me?'

'Every time. I won't sleep without mine now.'

'What about hotels?'

'I bring my board with me. Everywhere.'

That got home to me. I made my decision there and then.

'I'll get one tomorrow.'

'Good lateral thinking,' Laetitia said approvingly.

The young assistant in the DIY store was clearly fascinated by my request.

'I don't know anything about bad backs myself,' he said.

'You wouldn't,' I said, looking wistfully and enviously at his willowy figure.

'You're a big man,' he said. 'You'd need a strong board. Three-quarters of an inch thick, I'd say, or maybe the full inch.'

'Make it the full inch,' I said grandly.

'Actually, we're metric now,' he said coyly and blushed a little. 'It'll be 2.54 centimetres.'

'Good show,' I said, 'that'll impress them at home.'

'Would it be for a double bed?' he enquired delicately.

'There's a difficulty there,' I admitted. 'A single width board could cause problems for the party of the second part.'

Our minds were as one. Double width it would be. He produced a board, or rather, pointed one out to me.

'Could you help me carry it out to the car?'

It took the two of us all our strength to hoist it up on the roof rack. He looked doubtfully at it even after I had lashed it down in my best *Moby Dick* fashion.

'I haven't far to go,' I re-assured him.

He shook hands with me earnestly and wished me Godspeed. He seemed anxious on my behalf. Such a nice young man.

I backed the car right up to our front porch and lowered the board to the ground. Skinned knuckles and a big dent in the rear wing were nothing. I was fighting for a sciatica-free future. Dexterous levering brought the board leaning upright against the side wall of the porch. I rang the bell.

'You can take that thing away again. Now,' Madam said after one look.

'But you don't even know yet what it's for.'

'I know what it's not for and that's the inside of this house.'

Cathleen, our American visitor, came up from the kitchen. She eyed the board with interest.

'You-all putting in a new floor in the spare room or sumpin'?'

'It's a bed board,' I said. 'Very good for back trouble. Keeps your spine straight while you sleep.'

'Omigod,' she said and sat down on the hall chair. She seemed to be *choking. Not crying, surely?*

'That'll do my asthma no good,' she gasped.

'Bed boards are not for curing asthma,' I said testily. Really, these women! Asthma, I ask you?

'If you put that on the bed,' said Madam, 'we'll go right through the floor down to the cellar.' She turned around to go upstairs.

'Take it away,' she said over her shoulder.

Cathleen came out to the porch.

'You shouldn't do *this, Henry,' she said.*

She leaned against the board. Her shoulders were shaking.

'It cost me £45,' I said gloomily.

Cathleen helped me to hoist it up on the roof rack again.

'Ireland of the Welcomes,' she said mysteriously and began to laugh again. Immoderately.

The lissom young DIY assistant recognised me at once, even after all I'd been through since our first meeting. I didn't beat about the bush.

'Are you married?' I asked.

'Not actually.'

Not too clear, that answer. Wouldn't have satisfied Rumpole. Oh, the hell with Rumpole.

'I have the board back,' I said.

'I see that. The party of the second part?'

I nodded. 'The party of the second part.'

'Sorry, no cash refunds. I can only give you a credit note.'

That is why there is now £45 worth of best distemper in the garage. When next I met my false friend, the bogus explorer, I said:

'I'll have no more of your backchat, Laetitia.'

I told her why. She laughed in a way that reminded me of Cathleen and she didn't even enquire about my back.

I think I'll go and lie down for a while now.

10 Social Pleasures

Shortly after I retired, Proinsias MacAonghusa invited me to join himself, Tomás de Bhaldraithe and Art Ó Beoláin on walks in the Dublin mountains on Sunday afternoons. This very agreeable reunion with old friends was doubly welcome as it brought the opportunity of talking in Irish for a whole long afternoon in their lively company and so holding on to the fluency gained in my Gaeltacht days. And who better could anyone ask for than Tomás, Professor of Irish, of international renown as lexicographer, Proinsias, native speaker from Connemara, well-known author, journalist and prize-winning broadcaster, and Art, who added fluent French and Russian to his mellifluent Irish. We usually finished up with a few drinks in a favourite pub in Galloping Green. One afternoon as three elderly men sitting nearby rose to leave, one of them turned to us and said, 'We heard you talking the Irish. We couldn't understand a word but it was great to hear it.' And Prionsias recalled that on an earlier occasion in the same establishment when Art had joined them for the first time, he found he had no cash and proffered a cheque which the owner accepted without demur. Prionsias said to him, 'You've never seen our friend before and you took his cheque without question.' The owner replied 'I heard you talking always in Irish and I knew you were gentlemen.'

Later I joined them in the Dublin Oyster Society with Seán White, Louis Johnston and Paddy Corr. We had the oysters sent up from Galway and each of us was host to the others in due succession. We opened the oysters ourselves, proceeding somewhat jerkily as we laboured at our unaccustomed task. I don't want to reveal just how many dozen we ate, washed down with pints of Guinness, but those nights were (and still are) great fun. Over time the fell sergeant thinned our ranks but the vacancies were filled up quickly. Of the seven mentioned above, only Proinsias and myself remain, Art having retired to his native Kerry some twenty years ago. We are a varied lot, of differing backgrounds and occupations. None of us will willingly miss any of the eight oyster nights from September to April.

Friendship with Proinsias brought membership of Conradh na Gaeilge, of which he was President from 1989 to 1994. In 1993 he published a well-researched history of the organisation to mark its centenary. He inaugurated a programme of visits to the different Gaeltachts and we spent enjoyable days and nights on the Aran islands, Inis Oírr and Inis Meáin, at Ballinskelligs, Gougane Barra and An Rinn. This brought back memories of travels in Connemara and Donegal as Director of Gaeltacht Services but those were different experiences. I was on holiday now, free to spend hours walking the hills and by-ways and talking to local people. Irish is still strong, if far from widespread, in the places we visited, and there we savoured the indescribable atmosphere of what seemed a different world. On Inis Meáin we saw with some dismay that the house where J. M. Synge spent several summers, though still inhabited, was in poor repair and had a sad, neglected air. We were cheered and relieved to learn soon after that plans were well advanced to restore it.

We heard that some years previously when the Social Worker on the island was a nun, some of the women complained of the burden of their large families and hinted at contraception. But this practice was strictly forbidden by the Church and the good nun instructed them in the Billings Method, which was allowed. But the babies continued to arrive in the same large numbers and one mother observed sourly that the nun was the only one the Method seemed to work for.

On one of these trips I had the great good fortune to be able to land on Sceilg Mhicíl, a bare rock rising to a peak of 700 feet above the Atlantic, eight miles out from Ballinskelligs. Many have failed after frequent attempts, defeated by high seas, strong swells or torrential rains. Local boatmen often refuse to take visitors to the Skelligs even when the sea seems calm enough. They know too well the impossibility of landing when a swell is running, though the surge of the Atlantic seems unremarkable to the inexperienced visitor looking out from the mainland. Even Lloyd Praeger, who scorned dangers others drew back from, never succeeded, despite three attempts in mid-summer. On this rock a small community of monks lived a life of penitential austerity from the 9th to the 13th century, when they removed to the mainland at Ballinskelligs. Six beehive cells and two little oratories have survived the centuries, nestling on a rock shelf on the brow of a five-hundred-foot precipice. There are a few pockets of soil on which the monks may have grown herbs to vary their diet of seaweed, fish, shellfish from the rocks and sea-birds. Great flocks of gannets, fulmars and guillemots wheel and swoop above the rocks and the slightly comical-looking puffin emerges from his nest in a cleft to stare without fear at the visitor before taking off.

Words cannot convey the feeling evoked by climbing to the summit of Sceilg Mhicíl, seeing the evidence of the existence of a community of monks there a thousand years ago and gaining some notion of their way of life and the vision that brought them there.

Gougane Barra, St Finbarr's Hollow, in West Cork, is called after the saint who founded a monastery there in the 7th century. In it is a small, secluded mountain lake, source of the river Lee, bounded by precipitous mountains on all sides save the East. The abiding impression is of peace and calm and time standing still.

Another trip took us to Gort a'Choirce and Tory Island in July 2000 and, as on all of these outings, we had extraordinarily good weather. Years before I had made several fruitless attempts to set foot on Tory Island, eight miles off-shore in the Atlantic Ocean. A ferry that can accommodate about eighty passengers now provides a regular service but in the moderate sea prevailing we could have landed from any of the smaller boats. The King of Tory, Patsy Dan Rodgers welcomed us on the quay and gave us a brief account of how the islanders were threatened with evacuation to the mainland twenty years ago, but now have a new hotel, a proper ferry and a helicopter on call for emergencies. This was far from the poverty I remembered from my days with Gaeltacht Services.

When we set off for the mainland, the tide was so low that the ferry had to anchor some hundreds of yards off the pier and we were brought ashore in groups of twelve or so in the smaller boats. Each passenger was given a lifejacket and since the deck of the ferry was high above the small boat, we were let down overboard by two stalwarts of the crew and seized by two in the smaller boat who found seating for us. There were of course cheerful jokes about the *Titanic* and the absence of deck chairs.

Cumann Merriman, a society devoted to the memory of Brian Merriman and the history and literature of Thomond, was founded in 1967 by Con Howard, then in the Department of Foreign Affairs. I was one of the first members and have missed very few of the Summer and Winter Schools. The backbone of the Cumann is made up of Irish speakers of whom some, but not all, are or were members of Gael Linn, An Comhcaidreamh, or Conradh na Gaeilge. The Winter School is held in Irish, and at both Schools, impromptu sessions of Irish music and song continue far into the night. Both reflect the spirit of Merriman's *Cúirt an Mheán Oíche* and its earthy humour and ribald rhetoric and provide a focus for the re-union of old friends and kindred spirits.

I served as President of the Royal Victoria Eye and Ear Hospital from 1979 to 1981. The organisation appeared strange to me. The consultants seemed to run each his own fiefdom and the Matron ruled the nursing staff. The set-up in the three Dublin maternity hospitals, which have an international reputation seemed to me much better. The Master, himself a consultant, is appointed by the Governors and serves a term of seven years. He is, in effect, the CEO and has all the 'clout' of a leading consultant. The Eye and Ear is also a specialist hospital. The general hospitals may require a different regime.

On my first visits to the USA in the 1950s, like other visitors I was quickly impressed by how everything there dwarfed its European counterpart. The country itself is so huge, enormous distances separate cities. Buildings tower into the sky, every motor car seemed to be an outsize limousine. Even seaweed was on a giant scale, producing the giant *Macrosystis*, and in Portland, Maine I saw carrageen moss—still bearing its Irish name—as large as cabbage, the gatherers harvesting it from small boats, using rakes with handles twelve feet long. On a visit to Houston, Texas, at social gatherings where Texans stood around in talk, their height of six feet six (and some even taller) made me feel rather small at six feet, though at home that was enough to class you as a tall man.

While still a Director of Arramara, I was a delegate to International Seaweed symposiums held in Edinburgh, Galway, Santiago de Compostela, Spain, and Santa Barbara. Countries represented included Japan and the USA, both major producers of seaweed products, as well as most European countries, and papers were presented by leading scientists, both academic and industrial. In the late 1970s I attended a symposium in Santa Barbara hosted by the University of California at their 630-acre campus ten miles outside the town.

After several days of lectures, we were taken on a trip to San Diego Bay, to see a demonstration of the harvesting of *Macrosystis*.

This seaweed grows at depths of twelve to sixteen fathoms, with a stem 80–100 feet long and the large leaves spread out, floating on the surface of the water. They are reaped by a large barge equipped with a cutting mechanism on the stern which sails over the bed of kelp at a speed of two to three knots and mows the leaves at the rate of 70–80 tons per hour. A strong current of air operates to propel the cut weed into the hold of the vessel and in six hours, a cargo of 450 tons has been harvested.

I called at the town office one day looking for a map and heard a couple from New York enquiring about property prices. The husband had retired and they were greatly taken by Santa Barbara as well they might, and seriously considering settling there. All was going well until the husband got a sudden thought.

'What's this I hear about some San Andreas Fault?'

The town official shrugged.

'Well, they say it's there all right.'

'And liable to slip any time and cause an earthquake?'

'So they say.'

'Are the local people not worried all the time?'

The official laughed.

'Most of them I'd say are Zen Buddhists. They'd expect to enter on a new life as an eagle or a gazelle.'

The New Yorkers clearly didn't know what to make of his attitude, was he being flippant to show that he didn't really believe there was any serious danger, or was it so bad that he couldn't cope with it any other way? They thanked him and left. I looked at the official, he looked at me and we each knew without speaking what the other thought, 'They won't be back.'

When the Symposium was over, I decided to see more of California. When I told the manageress of the motel, a motherly woman in her fifties, that I was taking off for San Francisco, she asked me whether I had a warm pullover, because, she said, 'San

Francisco often has sudden heavy mists and they could give you a bad cold or even pneumonia.'

'But this is June,' I said. 'It's beautifully warm and dry and anyway, we're used to sudden changes of weather in Ireland.' But she was quite concerned.

'My son is in the East and won't be back for a month. He's about your size, I'd be happier if you'd take his jersey—you can mail it back to me when you leave for Ireland.' Before I could say another word she bustled off, came back with her son's jersey and would take no refusal.

I took the Greyhound bus to San Francisco timing myself to arrive in the main square in the early afternoon and went into what I had been told was the best hotel in the city, in the main square.

As I expected, there was no-one in the lobby at that hour except two young men behind the reception desk. They were two of those mannerly young people one meets in the States, very courteous, address every man over twenty-five as Sir. I looked around, admired the hotel, and it was genuine admiration and then said, 'I'm afraid it would be way above my budget, but I'd be much obliged if you could recommend me a good, small hotel, not too far from the centre of town, say around (naming a modest figure).' The elder of the two looked thoughtful, then said 'How long do you plan to stay in San Francisco Sir?'

'Three or four days.'

'Well, we have some staff on holiday just now and their rooms at the top of the house are vacant. They're small, but they might suit you. Would you like to see one?'

I said, 'Sure'. We went up in the elevator and from the top landing climbed the stairs to a short corridor, with rooms on both sides. He showed me one, small, yes, but it had a hand-basin, wardrobe, chest of drawers, a table, two chairs and a bed.

'There's a bathroom opposite. You'll have it all to yourself.'

'Suits me fine.'

As we went down to the lobby to collect my bag, I asked him 'What do I owe you for the room?'

He looked thoughtful again, then said, 'Would ten dollars a night be all right Sir?'

So there I was, lodged in the best, most luxurious hotel in the city, at a fraction of the normal cost. I had some people to contact and over a meal they had the usual question, 'Where are you staying?' and were visibly impressed when I told them, of course not saying that I was roosting in a small room way up under the roof. These two encounters were a refreshing antidote to my experience with the spoiled rich young group on my first visit to the USA in 1953. Jim Redington, the Gaeltara textile designer and I had embarked on the liner *United States*, flagship of the shipping line of that name. We sailed from Cobh and I was astounded at the great quantity of luggage, mostly cabin trunks, piled up on the tender that brought us out to the liner. The sea passage took five days but one arrived fresh, with the energy required to deal with Americans.

We travelled first-class and this meant dressing formally for dinner, with black tie. The other passengers were mostly Americans, senior executives with large corporations, with a small minority of obviously wealthy young men and women returning from a world cruise. A group of eight of these had a table near ours. The ship's orchestra discoursed popular music of the day and played afterwards in the adjoining salon when dancing began. On our second night, I made bold to ask one of the young women for a dance and met with a cold refusal and hostile looks from some of the men. I was completely taken aback, was this the democratic US of A? Everyone as good as his neighbour?

The third day out was a Sunday and Mass was celebrated in the steerage. The passengers there included many Irish and their cheerful, friendly company was very welcome after the somewhat stiff atmosphere in the first class. The next day I went to re-visit them but was stopped at a locked door by a crew member who told me politely but firmly that first-class passengers were not allowed into the steerage. These experiences took some of the shine off the luxury of the first class, with its food, equal to that in the finest restaurants ashore, its library, reading room, cinema, swimming pool and well-equipped state rooms.

On the whole, travel abroad on business, with the exception of attendance at international conferences, has not a great deal to recommend it. The people you must spend your time with, very often would not be your free choice for company. Meals with them can be tedious and your days and nights are fully occupied. The one advantage is that you can judge whether or not it would be worthwhile to return for a holiday.

It was certainly worthwhile visiting San Francisco, the steep streets, Chinese quarter with its doss-houses and alleged opium dens and the splendid harbour with its infamous prison island, Alcatraz.

On holiday travel, free from any work obligations, Patricia and I paid many visits to France, Portugal, Spain and Italy and spent several weeks in Houston, Texas, where Peter had an appointment as consultant and was also a professor in Texas University. All were enjoyable, but two stand out particularly in my memory, when Kato came with us to Barcelona and Vence. Her fluent Spanish, Italian and French were a great advantage and she also drove the car we hired.

In 1984, I shared a small hospital ward with Daniel Binchy, former Senior Professor in the School of Celtic Studies of the Institute for Advanced Studies. Our ailments were minor and did not prevent long conversations during our short stay. I remember two episodes he related from his past. 'When I was attending Bergin's classes to add to my scanty knowledge of Irish,' he said, 'a friend who was a native speaker from Kerry advised me strongly not to bother overmuch with text books but to go to the Gaeltacht and stay as long as I could, sharing the life of the local people and listening to them. So I went to Dunquin and spent months on the Great Blasket. The islanders spoke to me often about Robin Flower, the English scholar from the British Museum, who had been visiting the island since 1910. I knew something of Flower; he was an Oxford graduate, uncompromisingly English and a staunch Unionist. Despite this background, alien to their beliefs and way of life, the islanders had become very attached to him. They called him *Bláithín*, and one old man said to me, "*Neósfhainn do Bhláithín rudaí ná neósfhainn don sagart féin*", "I would tell Flower things I wouldn't tell to the priest himself."'

The second episode related to Binchy's time as first Irish Minister Plenipotentiary to Germany, from 1929 to 1932. The year after he took up his post in Berlin, Adolf Hitler's Nazis became the second largest party in the Weimar Republic, winning more than six million votes in the 1930 election. When the Cosgrave Government gave way to de Valera's first Fianna Fáil Government in March 1932, Binchy was recalled to Dublin for consultations.

He was taking leave of the Counsellor at the British Embassy, with whom he had become very friendly, when the Englishman enquired, 'When will we see you back here?' Binchy replied, 'I'm not sure about that, but I am sure about one thing, Adolf Hitler will be Chancellor of Germany within a year and the prospect of serving in his Germany is not very attractive to me.' The Englishman laughed at him. 'Marshal von Hindenburg would never allow that miserable little ex-corporal to become his Chancellor,' he said.

'Well,' said Binchy to me, 'I knew the real Germany better than the diplomat in his sheltered post. I had lived among students in Munich for three years and in Berlin I could drink with them in the beer cellars. My German was good, I could listen to the talk in the cafés and I had a good idea of what the Berliners thought about

Hitler and about President von Hindenburg, who was then eighty-six.'

'But my English friend persisted,' Binchy went on. 'He said to me, "The thing is impossible, Hitler to be Chancellor." I repeated, "Hitler will be Chancellor before another year." "Fifty pounds to a pound against you," said the Englishman. "Done," said I.'

Back in Dublin, Binchy decided to resign from the Diplomatic Service and return to the world of scholarship which he preferred. He watched events in Germany and as the talk in the cafés and beer cellars had predicted, President von Hindenburg was persuaded that Hitler and the Nazis could be controlled better within the Government than outside it and on 30 January 1933, he invited Hitler to be Chancellor. Binchy had won his bet.

Within a week a letter from Berlin arrived for him in the diplomatic bag and was duly forwarded. It contained a blank sheet of note paper bearing the crest of the British Embassy and a Bank of England note for fifty pounds. His English friend was a man of honour and diplomatic discretion.

In the summer of 1994 Kato had an English friend Maureen staying with her. I thought that a day out at Laytown Races would be amusing. Laytown is only six or seven miles from Drogheda and I had been to the races a few times as a schoolboy. So we set out on 4 August. The crowd attending was bigger than I remembered, but there were still the stalls of the thimble-rigger and the trick-of-the-loop man. The races were run on the strand—low tide left a fine expanse of level sand. The rectangular course was marked out with poles at strategic points and at the last half furlong to the finish the spectators stood behind a simple four foot wire fence and cheered on the horses thundering past within a few feet of them. The rest of the course was unfenced and spectators wandered along it or across it at their pleasure.

This August day turned out to be special. In the first race, the five-furlong Guinness Handicap, the leading horse, Five Little Girls, slipped in a stream after a furlong and brought down her immediate pursuer, Smart Rose, who broke her neck. Her jockey, Conor Everard, sustained a fractured collar bone and Mick Cleary, rider of Five Little Girls, had head injuries and also a fractured collar bone. This mayhem let the favourite come first, virtually unopposed. But the drama did not end there. Another horse, Tineran Rise, unseated her rider and galloped loose after passing the winning post. She then turned head-over-heels and also suffered fatal injuries. Robbie Burke, in attempting to pull up his mount, Galway Accent, collided with one of the local hunt horses, fracturing his wrist. So there were two horses killed and three jockeys rushed to hospital by the end of the first race.

The jockeys sent a deputation to the stewards and two of them accompanied stewards to the trouble spot which was a so-called refugee stream, left behind when the tide went out. The marked poles were re-arranged. Some horses were withdrawn from later races and there were many changes of jockey. The second race got under way after a half-hour's delay and started and finished without incident as did the third race. But in the fourth race, the St James' Gate Handicap, George Coogan's mount ducked suddenly off the course when a furlong and a half from the finish and he sustained a fractured wrist. There was more trouble in the fifth race, the Donnycarney Handicap, when the favourite, Lady Noble, was brought down by another horse and James Nash on Persian Tailor was unseated. His mount took off across the strand and was last seen heading for the Boyne Estuary in a mad gallop. He was found the next morning grazing peacefully on Baltray golf course, still with saddle and blinkers intact, having swum across the Boyne. When horses passed the finishing post as these incidents occurred, some began plunging around, to the great alarm of the spectators, but Committee men on horseback at the finishing post succeeded in bringing them under control very quickly, helped by men on foot seizing the reins.

The newspapers carried a full account of the races the next day, and the Turf Club announced their intention of carrying out an inquiry. Fortunately there were no reports of injuries to spectators, but it was clear that changes would have to be made to ensure their safety. Public concern increased and for a time it seemed that we had seen the last of the Laytown Races. But they were reprieved, the Turf Club relenting and agreeing they could carry on, but with stringent conditions about spectator safety, especially fencing.

When we moved to Dún Laoghaire I became a regular swimmer at the Forty-Foot in Sandycove, but only in the summer months, for Paddy Murray had cured me forever of cold weather swimming. In 1999 Radio Telefís Éireann produced a series called *Obsessions*, dealing with bird watchers, mountaineers and suchlike enthusiasts, delving into their motivation for their devotion to these somewhat esoteric activities. One programme in the series featured all-the-year-round swimmers at the Forty-Foot. An RTE film crew was sent to the Forty-Foot on a day in June that year and as it happened I came along the same day. The RTE did their filming unobtrusively and professionally to catch the swimmers in the normal relaxed manner. I was filmed walking into the Forty-Foot with my towel and togs under my arm and then in the water. Both shots were quite short and I was completely unaware that they were being taken.

Months later, at the end of October, the Forty-Foot programme was broadcast and it was naturally assumed that the film had been taken that month. I was immediately taken to be one of the all-the-year-round swimmers, congratulated on all sides and told what a great man I was, etc., etc. I was astonished at the number of friends and acquaintances who had seen the programme and what could I do but accept the accolades with becoming modesty? 'Shucks, it's nothing really!'

Envoi

Every avocation, even the most glamorous-seeming to outsiders, has its drawbacks and *longueurs* and in moments of depression, stress or numbing frustration one is tempted to agree with Henry David Thoreau of Concord, Massachusetts, that 'the mass of men lead lives of quiet desperation.' Then, fortunately, a chance encounter or a phone call, and you find yourself in lively company, the pints appear, the stories are good and are told with all the art of the seanchaí and life is worthwhile again.

Looking back over these memoirs, it might appear that I had an easy passage through life. The good times certainly were predominant, but it was not 'roses, roses all the way'. There were intervals of strain and worry, illnesses, operations, spells in hospital, sometimes of months, and periods of frustration and numbing boredom. We lost our first granddaughter, Róisín, at the age of twelve after a ten-year battle against leukaemia. And Willy, my eldest brother, having survived being blown up by a sea mine in the Mersey river and the torpedoing of a vessel in convoy in the Atlantic, died at sixty by misadventure in a Liverpool hospital. Other troubles seem of passing concern in comparison with these, which only time can alleviate and then only to a degree. No one, no family is immune from these blows of fate. They are an inescapable part of the human condition and you are wise to accept that life is unfair. I have long taken on board the wisdom of older people who reminded me from time to time that good health is a jewel of superlative value and 'as long as you have your health' you can cope with most situations and just get on with life.

Index of Names